Why Did?

12 Bible Stories You Thought You Knew

By
Tim Cummings
and LGC

ALTYRE PRESS
Nashville, TN

COPYRIGHT PAGE

For author bookings, bulk pricing information and additional support contact Altyre Press, 73 White Bridge Rd, Ste 103-211, Nashville, TN 37205

Phone: 615-945-2899

Blog: http://WhyDidStories.wordpress.com

Facebook: www.facebook.com/WhyDidStories

TABLE OF CONTENTS

PREFACE
By Steve Brown, Key Life Ministries

I've been teaching the Bible most of my adult life. At first I did it, because I was fairly certain that God told me to do it. It started with my own study. I was tired of hearing what others said about the Bible and decided to find out for myself. The truths I discovered became the anchor, the passion, and the "called" direction of my life.

That fact, to wit, a call to share with people the incredible truths that I had learned from my own study of Scripture, has been a privilege.

It has also been a place of difficulty and sometimes discouragement. I found out that people were not nearly as interested in the Bible as I was. So many just didn't care and, if they did, felt they were reading a book that was "above them" and one which they would never understand.

This book will blast the boredom to pieces and, for those who want to understand the Bible, open up a boatload of amazing possibilities and truths that will put legs on the reason God gave us the Bible in the first place.

My late friend and mentor, Fred Smith, was perhaps the wisest man I've ever known. He was also one of the most inquisitive men I've ever known. Fred grew up the son of a Baptist preacher and their family was "dirt poor." To add to the poverty, Fred had a withered hand which prevented him from participating in sports and, in some circles, brought derision. He was often lonely and, in that loneliness, would sometimes go out in the woods near his home. He told me once, "I thought then that there was something nobody was telling me and I determined to find out what it was."

For the rest of his life, Fred asked "Why?" about almost everything and that included the Bible.

As I read Tim and Grace Cummings' books, I began to see something that I had not seen before. I saw the necessary connection between Fred's asking "why?" and the amazing wisdom he had. His wisdom came from the Bible that he loved and taught and, interestingly, he got that wisdom by asking questions.

You hold in your hand a book that will change your life! With clarity and simplicity, (don't let the apparent "simplicity" fool you) this book will lead you into a whole new way of seeing and understanding the Bible.

Someone has said that the study of the Bible is like "peeling an onion", because one peels off layers and layers to only find more layers. I'm not sure that an "onion" is a proper metaphor for reading the Bible, but I do know that this book has revealed in a delightful way the layers and layers of profound truth that one can find in the Bible... truths that can be discovered by asking the simple question: Why?

Biblical Truth, however, is not an end in itself. You can know a whole lot of truth and if you just "know" it, it won't make much difference. The truth of the Bible serves only one purpose and that is to send us running to Jesus, the one who loves us far more than we can understand. This is a book about truth, how to discover it and, far more important, how to know the One who said, "I am the truth."

So get your Bible and let Tim and Grace Cummings take you to places where you've never been before, show you things you've never seen before, and make you think thoughts you've never thought before.

You will "rise up and call" them blessed and you will stand in awe of the God who has chosen to reveal Himself in the Scriptures.

Steve Brown is the teacher on *Key Life,* a syndicated radio program, an author and a professor at Reformed Theological Seminary in Orlando. His ministry Key Life (www.keylife.org) provides teaching and inspiration to millions. Steve has created the internet site PoopedPastors.com.

You can enjoy his on-line syndicated talk show SteveBrownEtc. at www.stevebrownetc.com.

You can learn more about Fred Smith at www.breakfastwithfred

ABOUT THIS BOOK

The book you hold in your hand is one of two volumes, penned by myself and my daughter, Grace. Both volumes will present God, His methods of operation, and the reliability of the relationship which He offers to you in ways you have not previously seen!

In 2005, Father placed upon my heart a desire to create a Bible study for young people who were old enough to study on their own and yet, young enough that their parents wished to be a part of their Christian education. As this idea took hold, I discussed it with my daughter who was 13 at the time. Grace had already displayed a personal relationship with Christ, a wonderfully inquiring mind, and a gift for writing. Together we developed the concept of a book written in two volumes – a book targeted for pre-teen and teenagers, with an accompanying volume for parents. I wrote the parents' volume and Grace rewrote the book for her age group. The basic volume will capture the interest of *anyone* curious of the Bible and God's working within it. The expanded version has additional material which the reader, a parent or teacher, can use in augmenting what is taught in the basic volume. Grace and I pray that these books will become a milestone in the development of strong believers across generational groupings within families.

ACKNOWLEDGEMENTS

Every good gift and every perfect gift is from above, coming down from the Father of lights with whom there is no variation or shadow due to change. James 1:17

Thanks to God for all of the innumerable gifts he has placed before me, especially my encouraging and loving family who fostered an understanding of faith within me from day one.

LGC

INTRODUCTION

As I started writing this book with my dad, I did not know many Bible stories in depth. I knew the basics - Noah and the Ark, Jesus' birth in a manger, etc., but nothing extensive. However, through this book I have not only learned facts about Bible stories, but I have come to know the author of them, His meaning, and the purpose of each.

God keeps repeating his plan of salvation to us throughout the whole Bible. He wants to have a personal relationship with you and wants you to know that He loves you. The Lord communicates this message to us in many ways, some simple and some complicated. It is a wonderful feeling when you finally just get it, grasp his message. So, my hope for you is that your experience in reading this book will as deeply impact you as it did me.

LESSON 1 – Why Did God Write the First Genealogy?

Definition

Genealogy: Genealogy is the history of you and your family. It is your mother and father, grandparents, great grandparents, and so on. It is often called "The Family Tree". You take the family and place them in order, called generations. Sometimes you have to do some tracking down for information, like in the family Bible or go to libraries, churches and even to the City Records building.

Culture

What is in a name? Have you ever thought about what a name means? In our recent past, many families had no last name. To identify themselves, they would use the term for their profession after their name. Often, the entire family would be involved in this trade or profession and soon, the term became a part of their name. See if you can match the name to the profession.

_A_ Baker	____	Metal Worker
_B_ Cooper	____	Wagon Maker
_C_ Smith	____	Barrel Maker
_D_ Wright	____	Bread Maker
_E_ Wainwright	____	Wood Worker

In the time of the Bible, all names had meaning. God has often used names, with their meanings, to communicate special information about His nature, His love and His plans for both His creation and His children.

The Bible has many genealogies printed in it. You probably know of the genealogy of Jesus that is part of the Gospels of Matthew or Luke. God uses these genealogies to show that Jesus was a descendent of King David and thus of the Royal line.

God uses genealogies in the Bible for many different purposes. Often as we read the long list of names (many of them we can't even say right) we may wonder why they are there. Let's read one example:

> GEN 5:1-32 This is the book of the generations of Adam. When God created man, he made him in the likeness of God. Male and female he created them, and he blessed them and named them Man when they were created.
>
> When Adam had lived 130 years, he fathered a son in his own likeness, after his image, and named him Seth. The days of Adam after he fathered Seth were 800 years; and he had other sons and daughters. Thus all the days that Adam lived were 930 years, and he died.
>
> When Seth had lived 105 years, he fathered Enosh. Seth lived after he fathered Enosh 807 years and had other sons and daughters. Thus all the days of Seth were 912 years, and he died.
>
> When Enosh had lived 90 years, he fathered Kenan. Enosh lived after he fathered Kenan 815 years and had other sons and daughters. Thus all the days of Enosh were 905 years, and he died.
>
> When Kenan had lived 70 years, he fathered Mahalalel. Kenan lived after he fathered Mahalalel 840 years and had other sons and daughters. Thus all the days of Kenan were 910 years, and he died.

When Mahalalel had lived 65 years, he fathered Jared. Mahalalel lived after he fathered Jared 830 years and had other sons and daughters. Thus all the days of Mahalalel were 895 years, and he died.

When Jared had lived 162 years he fathered Enoch. Jared lived after he fathered Enoch 800 years and had other sons and daughters. Thus all the days of Jared were 962 years, and he died.

When Enoch had lived 65 years, he fathered Methuselah. Enoch walked with God after he fathered Methuselah 300 years and had other sons and daughters. Thus all the days of Enoch were 365 years. Enoch walked with God, and he was not, for God took him.

When Methuselah had lived 187 years, he fathered Lamech. Methuselah lived after he fathered Lamech 782 years and had other sons and daughters. Thus all the days of Methuselah were 969 years, and he died.

When Lamech had lived 182 years, he fathered a son and called his name Noah, saying, "Out of the ground that the LORD has cursed this one shall bring us relief from our work and from the painful toil of our hands." Lamech lived after he fathered Noah 595 years and had other sons and daughters. Thus all the days of Lamech were 777 years, and he died.

After Noah was 500 years old, Noah fathered Shem, Ham, and Japheth.

Are your initial thoughts like mine once were? In 32 verses, we are introduced to 10 generations of fathers and sons. Other than the length of their lives, there seems to be little to be learned from this text. In fact, it would be very easy to skip this chapter completely and move on to chapter 6 about the corruption of mankind. What would we have missed? **WHY** did God include this genealogy of Adam in His Book? Let's look at what each name means.

Adam	**ADAM** m **Usage:** English, French, German, Polish, Russian, Romanian, Biblical **Pronounced:** A-dam Comes from *adomah*, and means "man."	Man אָדָם
Seth	**SETH (1)** m **Usage:** Biblical, English **Pronounced:** SETH Means "placed" or "appointed" in Hebrew. When he was born Eve said, "For God hath *appointed* me another seed instead of Abel, whom Cain slew."	Appointed שֵׁת
Enosh	**ENOSH m** **Usage: Biblical** **Pronounced: EE-nahsh** **From the root anash: to be incurable; used of a wound, grief, woe, sickness or wickedness.**	Mortal, Frail אֱנוֹשׁ

Kenan	**KENAN** m **Usage:** Biblical **Pronounced:** KEE-nan Possibly can mean sorrow, dirge, or elegy.	Sorrow קֵינָן
Mahalalel	**MAHLAH** f,m **Usage:** Biblical **Pronounced:** MAH-la, MAY-la from *mahalal*, which means "blessed" or "praise"; and *el*, the name for God. Thus, Mahalalel means "the Blessed God."	The Blessed God מֶהַלַלְל
Jared	**JARED** m **Usage:** English, Biblical **Pronounced:** JER-ed from the verb *yaradh*, meaning "shall come down."	Shall Come Down יָרֶד
Enoch	**ENOCH** m **Usage:** Biblical **Pronounced:** EE-nahk Enoch means "teaching," or "commencement." He was the first of four generations of preachers.	Teaching חֲנוֹך
Methuselah	**METHUSELAH** m **Usage:** Biblical **Pronounced:** me-THOOZ-e-la The name Methuselah comes from two roots: muth a root that means "death" ; and from shalach, which means "to bring," or "to send forth." Thus, the name Methuselah signifies, "his death shall bring."	His Death Shall Bring מות muth שלח shalach

Lamech	LAMECH m Usage: Biblical Pronounced: LAY-mek A root still evident today in our own English word, "lament" or "lamentation."	Despairing לֶמֶךְ
Noah	NOAH (1) m Usage: English, Biblical Pronounced: NO-a Noah is derived from nacham , "to bring relief" or "comfort,"	Comfort נֹחַ

If you look at these names and their meanings carefully, you find the plan of salvation in this first genealogy of the Bible:

For **man** [Adam] is **appointed** [Seth] **mortal** [Enosh] and to **sorrow** [Kenan], but **the blessed God** [Mahalalel] **shall come down** [Jared], **teaching** [Enoch] **His death shall bring** [Methuselah] to the **despairing** [Lamech], **comfort** [Noah].

God planned to redeem man even before He created mankind. In the Bible, God repeatedly presents this plan over and over in a variety of ways. Not everyone hears God in the same way, but God as the great communicator has transmitted His message in numerous ways. In Genesis 5, He uses a simple genealogy to show that He controls history. Even through the naming of generations of offspring, to communicate His wondrous plan to redeem us and restore us to our place of fellowship and relationship to Him.

My dad named my brother Timothy – Beloved of God. My dad has told me that he often thinks of this meaning when he thinks of my brother as he has grown into a young man. I would be surprised if any of his friends ever knew that this is what his name means.

In Bible times, everyone knew what names meant. Think of how Methuselah must have been teased because his name means "his death brings forth". Yet his father obeyed God in naming him. All of the fathers listed in this genealogy were used by God as they named their sons. Did they receive a word from God; did God just place the name in their mind? We don't know the answer to this. What we do know is that God had a plan. We know that God wanted us to know that plan. And, God used the names of 10 men at the beginning of His story to communicate in yet another way, the manner in which man would be reconciled to God.

Why does God give us the genealogy in Genesis Chapter 5? To show us that He loves us and has a plan to save us. A plan that is unchanged from the very beginning of creation! What a truly amazing God we have.

Prayer: Thank you, Father, for providing a plan of salvation and for communicating it to us in so rich a fashion. Thank you also for fathers who were faithful to name their sons according to Your perfect plan.

REFERENCES

Jones, Alfred. 1990. *Dictionary of Old Testament proper names.* Grand Rapids: Kregel Publications.

Kaplan, Rabbi Arveh. 1981. *The Living Torah.* Jerusalem: Maznaim Publishing Corporation.

Missler, Chuck. 1999. *Cosmic codes: Hidden messages from the edge of eternity.* Post Falls: Koinonia House.

Pink, Arthur W. 1922. *Gleanings in Genesis.* Chicago: Moody Bible Institute.

Rosenbaum, M. and Silbermann, A. 1973. *Pentateuch with Onkelas's translation (into Aramaic) and Rashi's commentary.* Jerusalem: Silbermann Family Publishers.

Stedman, Ray C. 1978. *The beginnings.* Waco: Word Books.

Answers to Culture Quiz

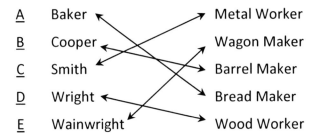

LESSON 1 NOTES:

LESSON 2 – **Why Did Abram Not Walk Through the Covenant with God?**

Definition

Covenant (Biblical):   While the word is used to identify treaties or similar contracts between rulers or individuals, the most important covenant in the Bible is the one between God and the Israelites (the Jews). This covenant was the basis for the Torah, and the claimed status of the Israelites as God's "chosen people." According to the terms of the covenant, Israelites understand that God had promised to undertake certain things on behalf of the people of Israel, and that the Israelites owed God obedience and worship in return.

The **Abrahamic Covenant** can be found in Genesis 15. In this covenant, God promises (see Genesis 12:1-3; 13:14-18; 15:1-21; 17:1-22):

1. To make the land of Abraham into a great nation;
2. To give Abraham many children;
3. To make Abraham a father of great many nations;
4. To bless Abraham and make him great;
5. To make Abraham a blessing to all the families of the earth;
6. To bless those who bless Abraham and curse those who curse him;
7. To give Abraham and his family all the land which he could see;
8. To give him a sign of the covenant (circumcision).

Culture

In the time of Abraham, to make a covenant required bloodshed. The parties of the covenant would sacrifice animals, walk together between the sacrifices, and say "may I be treated in the same way if I break my part of this agreement." Making covenants was a serious event, often performed in public with a great festival.

Let's read the story of Abram's covenant provided in Genesis 15.

Genesis 15

After these things the word of the LORD came to Abram in a vision: "Fear not, Abram, I am your shield; your reward shall be very great." But Abram said, "O Lord GOD, what will you give me, for I continue childless, and the heir of my house is Eliezer of Damascus?" And Abram said, "Behold, you have given me no offspring, and a member of my household will be my heir."

And behold, the word of the LORD came to him: "This man shall not be your heir; your very own son shall be your heir." And he brought him outside and said, "Look toward heaven, and number the stars, if you are able to number them." Then he said to him, "So shall your offspring be."

And he believed the LORD, and he counted it to him as righteousness.

And he said to him, "I am the LORD who brought you out from Ur of the Chaldeans to give you this land to possess." But he said, "O Lord GOD, how am I to know that I shall possess it?" He said to him, "Bring me a heifer three years old, a female goat three years old, a ram three years old, a turtledove, and a young pigeon." And he brought him all these, cut them in half, and laid each half over against the other. But he did not cut the birds in half. And when birds of prey came down on the carcasses, Abram drove them away. As the sun was going down, a deep sleep fell on

Abram. And behold, dreadful and great darkness fell upon him.

Then the LORD said to Abram, "Know for certain that your offspring will be sojourners in a land that is not theirs and will be servants there, and they will be afflicted for four hundred years. But I will bring judgment on the nation that they serve, and afterward they shall come out with great possessions. As for yourself, you shall go to your fathers in peace; you shall be buried in a good old age. And they shall come back here in the fourth generation, for the iniquity of the Amorites is not yet complete."

When the sun had gone down and it was dark, behold, a smoking fire pot and a flaming torch passed between these pieces. On that day the LORD made a covenant with Abram, saying, "To your offspring I give this land, from the river of Egypt to the great river, the river Euphrates, the land of the Kenites, the Kenizzites, the Kadmonites, the Hittites, the Perizzites, the Rephaim, the Amorites, the Canaanites, the Girgashites and the Jebusites."

In this very interesting passage, God promises Abram (note: God has not yet renamed him Abraham) both descendants and a land. He foretells of the exile to Egypt and then the return to this Promised Land. Abram believed God! To confirm this prophecy, God proposes a covenant with Abram.

God offers to join into a covenant with Abram. Abram is so excited! He gets the animals and kills them. He splits them up into quarters and lays them out on the ground. And then he waits for God to show up.

How long does he have to wait? Well, so long that vultures start to circle the pieces of meat. He has to spend his day shooing them away. The sun gets hot, and Abram starts to swelter in the heat. God does not appear. The sun moves across the sky, midday passes, the day advances. As dusk is settling in, we find that God places Abram in a deep sleep – *a thick and dreadful darkness*.

After Abram's faithfulness in waiting through the heat of the day, **why did** *God cause him to fall asleep?*

Remember the premise of the covenant - two parties meeting as equals? How can a sinful man ever face God as an equal? God appears to establish his covenant with Abram – but it is not a covenant between equals. God comes as a smoking pot and a flaming brand. Alone, without Abram, He passes between the animal sacrifices. ***Why?***

By passing alone between the animals, God could have been saying that Abram had no part in this covenant, and that he and his descendants were excluded. If this was God's intention, then there was no contract or agreement between God and Abram and therefore no accountability for breaking the covenant. But why then even have a covenantal ceremony?   There would be no purpose – and God, if anything, is a God of purpose!

By passing through the sacrificed animals alone, God was not only affirming the covenant, but He was stating that regardless of who might break the covenant, that He alone would bear the punishment should the covenant be broken.

What were the terms for Abram? Abram was called to believe in God - to place his trust and his faith in all that God promised, never failing to trust and walk in the way of the Lord. Did Abram live up to his side of the covenant? Even after God promised to give him a son Abram got impatient and tried to do it on his own! Abram's relationship with Sarah's handmaiden resulted in their son, Ishmael. While God honored His promise and made Ishmael a great nation, he was not the child of the covenant!

From God's actions, we can see that He considered the covenant as a reality. By passing alone between the quartered animals, God assumed upon himself, all accountability for any breaking of the covenant –*by either party!* Abram was not excluded but he was relieved of accountability. God declared that God alone would pay the price.

Here we have stated that regardless of who breaks the covenant God made with Abram (and his descendants) God will bear the punishment. Take a look at Luke 22:39-44

> And he came out and went, as was his custom, to the Mount of Olives, and the disciples followed him. And when he came to the place, he said to them, "Pray that you may not enter into temptation." And he withdrew from them about a stone's throw, and knelt down and prayed, saying, "Father, if you are willing, remove this cup from me. Nevertheless, not my will, but yours, be done." And there appeared to him an angel from heaven, strengthening him. And being in an agony he prayed more earnestly; and his sweat became like great drops of blood falling down to the ground.

Christ is in the Garden of Gethsemane entering into His passion. In this prayer, Jesus is petitioning God, the Father, to permit the punishment ahead to pass from Him (*let this cup pass...*). God's answer to this prayer is a resounding <u>NO</u>!

Why? In Genesis 15, God passed between the quartered animals by Himself promising to bear the punishment if Abram or his descendants broke their side of the covenant – to be faithful to God. Abram and all his descendants have broken this covenant of faithfulness. In that moment in the Garden of Gethsemane, God (the Son) chose to pay the price – to shed His blood and give up His life to uphold the covenant made by God the Father.

Jesus went on to the cross, and there, He paid for all of our sins. While on the cross he said, "It is Finished". He used the Greek verb *teleo*, which means **paid in full**. Jesus paid for all of our sins in full.

Now we can see **why** it was that Abram did not pass between the sacrifices of the covenant with God. In Genesis 15, an all-knowing God chose to place His Son at risk to pay for man's inability to keep covenant with God.

Prayer: Thank you, Father, for Your faithfulness in the face of Abraham's and our own inability to keep covenant with You. Thank you for paying the price of the broken covenant and for paying our debt in full.

REFERENCES

Beers, V. Gilbert.1980. *The Book of Life, Vol 1.Grand Rapids:* The Zondervan Corporation
Retrieved from http://www.answers.com/topic/covenant-biblical?method=6 (Definition of Covenant)

LESSON 2 NOTES:

LESSON 3 – Why Did God Give Detailed Instructions for Decorating the Golden Lampstand?

Definition

Wrought: Shaped by hammering with tools. Used chiefly of metals or metalwork. (American Heritage Dictionary)

Culture

In the ancient world, there were no candles to provide light at night. People would burn oils, such as olive oil, in lamps to have light. Lamps were often made from clay or various metals, having a bowl to hold the oil and a spout to hold the wick. The oil in the lamp would soak up through the wick, and when the wick was lit, the oil would burn, providing light.

In the Tabernacle, the Golden Lampstand had seven arms. On top of each arm rested a golden lamp. The priests would light these lamps at dusk and allow them to burn all night. At dawn, each lamp would be extinguished; the oil would be replenished with special sacred oil; and the wicks would be trimmed so that the lamps were ready to be used again at dusk.

Let's read the story provided in Exodus 25:31-40.

> "Make a lampstand of pure gold and hammer it out, base and
> shaft; its flowerlike cups, buds and blossoms shall be of one
> piece with it. Six branches are to extend from the sides of the

lampstand - three on one side and three on the other. Three cups shaped like almond flowers with buds and blossoms are to be on one branch, three on the next branch, and the same for all six branches extending from the lampstand. And on the lampstand there are to be four cups shaped like almond flowers with buds and blossoms. One bud shall be under the first pair of branches extending from the lampstand, a second bud under the second pair, and a third bud under the third pair - six branches in all. The buds and branches shall all be of one piece with the lampstand, hammered out of pure gold. "Then make its seven lamps and set them up on it so that they light the space in front of it. Its wick trimmers and trays are to be of pure gold. A talent of pure gold is to be used for the lampstand and all these accessories. See that you make them according to the pattern shown you on the mountain." (TLB)

THE GOLDEN CANDLESTICK

A drawing from a Tabernacle Shadowbook printed in 1946

In this section, God is giving Moses instructions for making the Lampstand which would light His Tabernacle. The Lampstand would provide light for the priests as they ministered before God. Let's look at the description of this special piece of furniture.

The lampstand was made from a single talent of gold. A talent of gold was approximately 120 pounds of pure gold. It was a wrought or beaten work. This means the lampstand was not made in pieces and then put together; instead, the various parts were actually formed by hammering the shapes and features out of a single slab of gold. This Lampstand was the only piece of furniture in the Tabernacle made of pure gold and the only beaten work. These two features point to Christ. The gold represents that Christ is God. The beaten nature of the lampstand shows how He would suffer for our sins.

We see that the lampstand had seven places for holding lamps. There was a center post from which three arms came out of each side. Each arm as well as the center post had a place for a lamp. We see this same design in the Jewish Menorah.

Considering the decorations on the Lampstand, the central stem and each of its branches were decorated with symbols of the three stages of the almond tree's life which were the bud, the flower, and the ripened fruit. The significance of the almond is that it is an emblem of resurrection and regeneration.

Many people point to the Lampstand as representing Christ as the *light of the world*. Dr. Arthur W. Pink, a most knowledgeable source of information on the Tabernacle, disagrees with this statement. **Why?**

Once again, let's look to the scriptures and try to find God's clear meaning. Look at John 9:3-5

Jesus answered, "It was not that this man sinned, or his parents, but that the works of God might be displayed in him. We must work the works of him who sent me while it is day; night is coming, when no one can work. As long as I am in the world, I am the light of the world."

This is a very explicit statement. Jesus claimed to be the Light of the World only while He was here. To clarify this statement even more, Christ said to His disciples in John 12:35-36

So Jesus said to them, "The light is among you for a little while longer. Walk while you have the light, lest darkness overtake you. The one who walks in the darkness does not know where he is going. While you have the light, believe in the light, that you may become sons of light." When Jesus had said these things, he departed and hid himself from them.

We see the image as Christ as the Light of the World being limited to His time on earth. So, what does the Lampstand represent? *Why* is it important to us today? And why did God provide so much detail regarding how it was to be decorated? If we consider how it was used, we will gain additional insight. Let's see when the lamps were actually burned. In Leviticus 24:2-3 we read:

"Command the people of Israel to bring you pure oil from beaten olives for the lamp, that a light may be kept burning regularly. Outside the veil of the testimony, in the tent of meeting, Aaron shall arrange it from evening to morning before the LORD regularly. It shall be a statute forever throughout your generations. He shall arrange the lamps on the lampstand of pure gold before the LORD regularly."

The lamps on the Lampstand burned from dusk until dawn, providing light during the hours of darkness. Remember that

Christ spoke distinctly about the period of darkness, the time when He is absent from us. So, the Lampstand is key to the time between Christ's first and second comings.

We can see that the Lampstand is a tool to benefit the priests as they perform their duties before God. We also see that it was employed during the hours of darkness. **Why** are we given *this level of detail*? Perhaps, there is more that God wants us to understand about this symbol for the time between Christ's two physical appearances on earth.

The decorations consist of clusters representing three distinct objects – the bud, the flower and the fruit of the almond. On the center stalk, there are four separate expressions of this cluster, resulting in 12 distinct objects (4 buds, 4 flowers, and 4 fruits). On each arm, there were three groups of three items or 9 distinct representations of the almond. If we take the center stalk and three arms of the Lampstand, we count a total of 39 separate representations of the almond. This leaves us with three more arms or another 27 representations of the almond. So, God expressly described a total of 66 representations of the almond to appear on the Lampstand. These representations were beaten or hammered out from the single piece of gold. They were not fashioned separately and then fastened on to the Lampstand to decorate it. They were part of the whole!

Do these numbers sound familiar? There are 39 books in the Old Testament. In the New Testament we have 27 books, for a total of 66 books. Consider the claim of the Bible as the inspired Word of God. Each of the books is taken from the single, universal truth of God. They are fashioned from God's truth, not written separately and then "stuck together" to make a book. Could it be that the

Golden Lampstand is an image of the Bible, Old and New Testaments?

Christ talks about us needing the light to see how to do God's will when it is dark – that is when He is gone from our midst. This is clearly the purpose of God's written word. The light from the Lampstand was available only to the priest ministering before God. We are told in scripture that to the lost, the scriptures will appear as foolishness. Those born a second time, serve as the living priesthood. We serve before the Lord, with His Word instructing us and illuminating the tasks He lays before us. Remember that when Christ returns, we will see clearly and the need for His word (the Lampstand) will cease as we bask in His light.

So, in the space of a few short verses in Exodus, God provides a very interesting portrayal of what will, in the future, become the Bible, His divinely inspired word. Sixty-six books, written by various writers over several thousand years, and yet one truth, one unity, beaten from the very gold of His truth, to light our path until His return.

Prayer: Thank you, Father, that You cared enough about us to go to great detail, even to the decorations on a lampstand that we might know we can trust in Your Word. May Your Word, the Bible, illuminate our daily walk with You until You return to earth.

REFERENCES

Cummings, Thomas L. 1988. *Study of the Tabernacle.* (Unpublished).
Pink, Arthur W. 1981. *Gleanings from Exodus.* Chicago: Moody Press.

LESSON 3 NOTES:

LESSON 4 – Why Did David Take Five Smooth Stones?

Definition

Sling: a device made of leather and other materials used to catapult stones or other objects at an enemy. Slings varied in length according to circumstances, the shorter ones were used in the assault upon captured towns and the longer to shoot an enemy from a distance. Stones or bullets could be projected from a sling to greater distance than either arrows from a bow or javelins. The projectiles used in slings were in earlier times smooth pebbles, but afterwards leaden bullets; they were carried either in a bag (in Greek, *marsupium*), or in the outer clothes.

Culture

Consider David's weapon, the sling. While today, we think little of such a toy, it was actually a very significant weapon in the hands of a well-trained warrior. The slingers occupied a far more honorable position in the Israelite armies than in those of the Greeks and Romans. The value which the Israelites assigned to the sling as an engine of destruction may also be estimated from the frequent use in the prophecies of the expression to "sling-out" a people, a term to mean total extermination.

Let's read the story provided in I Samuel 17 (selected verses):

> Now the Philistines gathered their armies for battle. And they were gathered at Socoh, which belongs to Judah, and encamped between Socoh and Azekah, in Ephes-dammim. And Saul and the men of Israel were gathered, and encamped in the Valley of Elah, and drew up in line of battle against the Philistines. And the Philistines stood on the

mountain on the one side, and Israel stood on the mountain on the other side, with a valley between them.

And there came out from the camp of the Philistines a champion named Goliath of Gath, whose height was six cubits and a span. He had a helmet of bronze on his head, and he was armed with a coat of mail, and the weight of the coat was five thousand shekels of bronze. And he had bronze armor on his legs, and a javelin of bronze slung between his shoulders. The shaft of his  spear was like a weaver's beam, and his spear's head weighed six hundred shekels of iron. And his shield-bearer went before him. He stood and shouted to the ranks of Israel, "Why have you come out to draw up for battle? Am I not a Philistine, and are you not servants of Saul? Choose a man for yourselves, and let him come down to me. If he is able to fight with me and kill me, then we will be your servants. But if I prevail against him and kill him, then you shall be our servants and serve us." And the Philistine said, "I defy the ranks of Israel this day. Give me a man, that we may fight together." When Saul and all Israel heard these words of the Philistine, they were dismayed and greatly afraid.

For forty days the Philistine came forward and took his stand, morning and evening. And Jesse said to David his son, "Take for your brothers an ephah of this parched grain, and these ten loaves, and carry them quickly to the camp to your brothers.

And he came to the encampment as the host was going out to the battle line, shouting the war cry. And Israel and the Philistines drew up for battle, army against army. And David left the things in charge of the keeper of the baggage and ran to the ranks and went and greeted his brothers. As he talked with them, behold, the champion, the Philistine of Gath, Goliath by name, came up out of the ranks of the Philistines and spoke the same words as before. And David heard him….

And David said to Saul, "Let no man's heart fail because of him. Your servant will go and fight with this Philistine." And Saul said to David, "You are not able to go against this Philistine to fight with him, for you are but a youth, and he has been a man of war from his youth." But David said to Saul, "Your servant used to keep sheep for his father. And when there came a lion, or a bear, and took a lamb from the flock, I went after him and struck him and delivered it out of his mouth. And if he arose against me, I caught him by his beard and struck him and killed him. Your servant has struck down both lions and bears, and this uncircumcised Philistine shall be like one of them, for he has defied the armies of the living God." And David said, "The LORD who delivered me from the paw of the lion and from the paw of the bear will deliver me from the hand of this Philistine."

And Saul said to David, "Go, and the LORD be with you!"

Then he took his staff in his hand and chose five smooth stones from the brook and put them in his shepherd's pouch. His sling was in his

David took his stones from the Brook of Elah

hand, and he approached the Philistine…. And when the

Philistine looked and saw David, he disdained him, for he was but a youth, ruddy and handsome in appearance.

And the Philistine said to David, "Am I a dog that you come to me with sticks?" And the Philistine cursed David by his gods. The Philistine said to David, "Come to me, and I will give your flesh to the birds of the air and to the beasts of the field."   Then David said to the Philistine, "You come to me with a sword and with a spear and with a javelin, but I come to you in the name of the LORD of hosts, the God of the armies of Israel, whom you have defied.   This day the LORD will deliver you into my hand, and I will strike you down and cut off your head. And I will give the dead bodies of the host of the Philistines this day to the birds of the air and to the wild beasts of the earth, that all the earth may know that there is a God in Israel, and that all this assembly may know that the LORD saves not with sword and spear. For the battle is the LORD's, and he will give you into our hand."

When the Philistine arose and came and drew near to meet David, David ran quickly toward the battle line to meet the Philistine.   And David put his hand in his bag and took out a stone and slung it and struck the Philistine on his forehead. The stone sank into his forehead, and he fell on his face to the ground.   So David prevailed over the Philistine with a sling and with a stone, and struck the Philistine and killed him. There was no sword in the hand of David.   Then David ran and stood over the Philistine and took his sword and drew it out of its sheath and killed him and cut off his head with it. When the Philistines saw that their champion was dead, they fled.   And the men of Israel and Judah rose with a shout and pursued the Philistines as far as Gath and the gates of Ekron, so that the wounded Philistines fell on the way from Shaaraim as far as Gath and Ekron

Here we have a Bible story that is known by young and old alike. We watch as David, recently anointed by Samuel to be king in place of Saul, makes his first entry into public service. He is still a young man, tending to his father's sheep. He is hardly anything of which to take note. As the youngest of the family, he becomes the messenger, delivering *care packages* to his three brothers serving in Saul's army.

At the time of our story, the army of the Philistines was facing the army of the Israelites across the Valley of Elah. The Philistines had a secret weapon. Their army had giants. We find that the champion of the Philistines was Goliath of Gath. And he was truly a *secret weapon*.

According to this passage, Goliath was over 9 feet tall. His armored breastplate weighed 150 pounds and the head of his spear weighed more than 19 pounds. Twice, daily he would come forth and issue his challenge to the Israelites across the valley. The timing of his challenge was calculated to interfere with the morning and evening prayers. His challenge intentionally took the

Israelites' attention away from God, their strength and their refuge and focused their attentions on the *inevitable* defeat that was to come should any Israelite take up Goliath's challenge. I am sure as he stood there; every soldier of the army of Israel believed that Goliath was unbeatable.

A view of the Valley of Elah

This stalemate continued for 40 days. We know from Biblical numerology that the number 40 represents a period of testing or trial. David arrives in the camp. Hearing the clamor of Goliath's challenge, he runs to the front lines to see what is going on. He hears the challenge and asks why no one will go forth to deal with this uncircumcised infidel. His older brother chides him. What does David know? He is not a soldier. He doesn't understand military things. He is just a shepherd boy running groceries to his brothers. Just like an older brother isn't it?

And yet, David does what no one in the camp of Israel has done. He changes the problem from a military one to a spiritual one. He knows that the Living God of Israel has it all over the Philistine idol, Dagon. From this point on, for David, the outcome is never in doubt. David persists and soon he is brought to the attention of the king. Saul summons David into his presence and David proceeds to volunteer to take out Goliath. Saul is, I am sure, enjoying the humor of the moment.

Then, David lays out his credentials. First, he is a shepherd who must protect his father's sheep from predators. Second, he has killed not only a bear, but also a lion. These feats must have impressed Saul, who probably had hunted lions for sport – from a chariot with spears and with other men to help. Finally, David lays out his most significant credential – his absolute trust in God to not only protect David, but to show His own power over an uncircumcised Philistine. Is such faith your greatest credential?

This appeal, which most of us would have viewed as false bravado, struck a chord with Saul. Perhaps he remembered his own call to serve God. When we consider his uncertainty, now, before God, we can believe that Saul responded to the surety displayed by

David and his transparent faith in God. His response to David is short and to the point. Go and the Lord be with you!

As David goes forth to face Goliath, he pauses by the brook of Elah and selects five smooth stones. Then he runs forward to meet Goliath's challenge. Goliath is obviously insulted that they would send a *boy* to do a *man's* job. He vows to make short work of this upstart, and then looks forward to enslaving the rest of the army. Goliath has no doubt that he will be victorious over David.

The long anticipated battle between champions begins. Goliath, the giant, incited to anger, lumbers forth in his armor with his shield and javelin. David, stripped down, quick of foot and lithe of limb, veritably dances before Goliath. Can you imagine Goliath yelling at David to just stand still? David keeps dancing, and finally, when Goliath fully faces him, David lets a stone from the brook fly. As we have been shown by the narrative, his hours and days spent with the sheep, permitted him to develop deadly accuracy. The stone lodges in the middle of Goliath's forehead and he comes crashing forward to the ground.

Goliath the champion of Dagon is dead. Once again, God has defended His own champion. David rushes forward to draw Goliath's own sword and cuts off the giant's head as a trophy to the Lord. God then strikes fear in the hearts of the Philistines and the army of Israel pursues and destroys their enemies.

So goes the well-known story of David and Goliath. But as you know, this is a book of **why.** So here is the question. **Why** does David take five stones from the brook before he goes to face Goliath? The Bible is very specific as to the number and the quality of these projectiles. Let's look at another passage from 2 Samuel which refers to the time after Saul's death.

II Samuel 21:14-22 And they buried the bones of Saul and his son Jonathan in the land of Benjamin in Zela, in the tomb of Kish his father. And they did all that the king commanded. And after that God responded to the plea for the land.

There was war again between the Philistines and Israel, and David went down together with his servants, and they fought against the Philistines. And David grew weary. And Ishbi-benob, one of the descendants of the giants, whose spear weighed three hundred shekels of bronze, and who was armed with a new sword, thought to kill David. But Abishai the son of Zeruiah came to his aid and attacked the Philistine and killed him. Then David's men swore to him, "You shall no longer go out with us to battle, lest you quench the lamp of Israel."

After this there was again war with the Philistines at Gob. Then Sibbecai the Hushathite struck down Saph, who was one of the descendants of the giants. And there was again war with the Philistines at Gob, and Elhanan the son of Jaare-oregim, the Bethlehemite, struck down Goliath the Gittite, the shaft of whose spear was like a weaver's beam. And there was again war at Gath, where there was a man of great stature, who had six fingers on each hand, and six toes on each foot, twenty-four in number, and he also was descended from the giants. And when he taunted Israel, Jonathan the son of Shimei, David's brother, struck him down.

These *four* were descended from the giants in Gath, and they fell by the hand of David and by the hand of his servants.

From this passage in II Samuel we learn some interesting facts. In addition to Goliath, there were four other giant of Gath encountered by David and his *might men*. One of these other giants also carries the name of Goliath, but was killed by David's nephew. These four giants were relatives of Goliath. Perhaps, the fact that there were four giants in addition to Goliath who fought for the Philistines is a clue to David's actions.

In Biblical numerology, the number 5 represents *grace*. In this story of David, we see him, as he prepares to face Goliath, arm himself to take on the other four giants as well. In his faith, David, believing that after God uses him to kill Goliath he might have to fight and kill these four relatives as well, picks up five stones from the brook. Armed with these five smooth stones, he goes forth confidently to face the champion from Gath.

Even though David was prepared, God in His grace struck the entire Philistine army with fear and they ran away. The Israelites pursued them and completed the prophesy that David proclaimed regarding the fate of the Philistine army.

Prayer: Father, I remember Your faithfulness to provide us with the skills we need to face life's challenges. I commit to exercise these gifts, even in my solitude, so that they can become *deadly* in their effectiveness. Finally, as I face my daily challenge, arm me to accomplish the full measure of the challenge placed before me.

REFERENCES

Bolan, Todd. Elah Valley from Azekah. *BiblePlaces.com.* Retrieved from
http://www.Bibleplaces.com/images/Elah_Valley_from_Azekah_tb_n02220
1.jpg

Bolen, Todd. Elah Brook with Students Picking Smooth Stones. *BiblePlaces.com.*
Retrieved from
http://www.Bibleplaces.com/images/Elah_brook_with_students_picking_s
mooth_stones_75-03tb.jpg .

Hawkins. Walter. Observations on the Use of the Sling as a Warlike Weapon
Among the Ancients. Retrieved from http:// www.Slinging.org/30.html.

Schindler, Oscar. David und Goliath, a colour lithograph c. 1888.

LESSON 4 NOTES:

LESSON 5 – Why Did the Hand Write on the Wall?

Definition

Stele: An upright stone or slab with an inscribed or sculptured surface, used as a monument or as a commemorative tablet in the face of a building.

Culture

In ancient times, rulers would surround themselves with advisors. Many of these advisors would give advice to their rulers based on fortune telling and interpretation of dreams. Often, the advisors' predictions were filled with double meanings. That way, no matter what happened, the advisors could say that their visions were correct and that the person hearing it had misinterpreted what they had said. It is important to note that the Bible prohibits believers from engaging in any type of fortune telling. However, there are numerous accounts in the Bible of God giving His chosen representatives the ability to foretell the future. These individuals were prophets. One sign of a true prophet - he had to be 100% right all of the time.

There are people today that say they can tell you the future. Christians have no need for such fortune telling. We depend on and trust in God's sovereignty over our lives. Nothing will ever happen to us that He does not know about and give us the strength to bear. How can you tell if the prophecy comes from

God or if it is from a false prophet? Does the prophecy get people to look to God and trust in Him, or does it tend to take them away from trusting in him and cause them to depend on their own abilities or even worse to depend on the person telling their fortune?

The Dating Controversy

The controversy over dating deals with *when* this book was written. Some historians and scholars do not believe that the Book of Daniel was actually written by him at the time of the Jewish exile to Babylon. The people, who believe that Daniel actually wrote this book, believe that he recorded the events before they happened based on what God told him. This would make Daniel a true prophet and all of his prediction, by definition, would have to be 100% accurate.

Those who support the later writing of this book, don't believe in prophesy and so believe that the accounts of the book must have been written after the actual events occurred. These doubters of prophesy believe that many of the events to which Daniel refers surround the rise to power of Antiochus Epiphanes 175-163 BC, and that the Book of Daniel was written by an unknown author of this period.

Perhaps we can use the question **why** to resolve this issue of dating the writings of this book. Let's examine one of the more unique passages of Daniel.

DANIEL 5 (Selected Verses) King Belshazzar made a great feast for a thousand of his lords and drank wine in front of the thousand. Belshazzar, when he tasted the wine, commanded that the vessels of gold and of silver that Nebuchadnezzar his father had taken out of the temple in Jerusalem be brought, that the king and his lords, his wives, and his concubines might drink from them. Then they brought in the golden vessels that had been taken out of the temple, the house of God in Jerusalem,

DANIEL INTERPRETING THE WRITING ON THE WALL
In the same hour came forth fingers of a man's hand, and wrote over against the candlestick upon the plaster of the wall of the king's palace   MENE, MENE, TEKEL, UPHARSIN.   (Daniel 5.5, 25)

and the king and his lords, his wives, and his concubines drank from them. They drank wine and praised the gods of gold and silver, bronze, iron, wood, and stone.

Immediately the fingers of a human hand appeared and wrote on the plaster of the wall of the king's palace, opposite the lampstand. And the king saw the hand as it wrote. Then the king's color changed, and his thoughts alarmed him; his limbs gave way, and his knees knocked together. The king called loudly to bring in the enchanters, the Chaldeans, and the astrologers. The king declared to the wise men of Babylon, "Whoever reads this writing, and shows me its interpretation, shall be clothed with purple and have a chain of gold around his neck and shall be the third ruler in the kingdom."

Then all the king's wise men came in, but they could not read the writing or make known to the king the interpretation....

Then Daniel was brought in before the king. The king answered and said to Daniel, "You are that Daniel, one of the exiles of Judah, whom the king my father brought from Judah. I have heard of you that the spirit of the gods is in you, and that light and understanding and excellent wisdom are found in you. Now the wise men, the enchanters, have been brought in before me to read this writing and make known to me its interpretation, but they could not show the interpretation of the matter. But I have heard that you can give interpretations and solve problems. Now if you can read the writing and make known to me its interpretation, you shall be clothed with purple and have a chain of gold around your neck and shall be the third ruler in the kingdom."

Then Daniel answered and said before the king, ... this is the writing that was inscribed: MENE, MENE, TEKEL, and PARSIN. This is the interpretation of the matter: MENE, God has numbered the days of your kingdom and brought it to an end; TEKEL, you have been weighed in the balances and found wanting;
PERES, your kingdom is divided and given to the Medes and Persians."

Then Belshazzar gave the command, and Daniel was clothed with purple, a chain of gold was put around his neck, and a proclamation was made about him, that he should be the third ruler in the kingdom. That very night Belshazzar the Chaldean king was killed. And Darius the Mede received the kingdom, being about sixty-two years old.

Why do we have this famous story of the handwriting on the wall? The mention of Belshazzar as the last king of Babylon in Daniel 5:30 seemed to be an error to many historians and critics. They claimed that Nabonidus was the last king of Babylon. Yet here in this passage, the writer makes it clear that the ruler of Babylon at the time of its fall was Belshazzar.

We have the report of an event where Belshazzar holds a great feast. To make sure the party is a big hit, he has his servants bring out the treasures from Solomon's temple which were captured during the destruction of Jerusalem in 606 BC. He and his guests are eating from the trays and drinking from the cups that were once consecrated to the worship of God in His Holy Temple. While they partied, they offered up toasts to all of their idol gods. What Belshazzar did not know was that his party would become the talk of the town!

In the midst of the party, a mysterious hand appears from thin air. This hand inscribes four words on the wall of the banquet hall. The four words, MENE, MENE, TEKEL, PARSIN, could not be understood by anyone at the feast. In the midst of the fear and confusion caused by this sight, Belshazzar calls for all of his wise men. He promises to whoever can read the writing on the wall a purple robe, a gold chain, and a promotion to be the third highest ruler of the kingdom. Despite these promised riches and honors, none of the wise men could translate the handwriting on the wall.

One of Belshazzar's wives remembers another wise man. Daniel, who could be well into his eighties, is no longer active in government service; but his reputation is still well known and comes to the mind of Belshazzar's wife. Even though out of the spotlight of power, Daniel's godly reputation continues to be known and spread throughout Babylon.

Daniel comes when summoned. He tells Belshazzar to keep his rewards; he will reveal the meaning of the message. The hand has written *Mene*: God has numbered the days of your reign and brought it to an end. *Tekel*: You have been weighed on the scales and found wanting. *Peres*: Your kingdom is divided and given to the Medes and Persians.

And, according to history, this very thing happened that same night. The Medo-Persian army stopped the flow of the Euphrates River. They then entered Babylon by pushing open the gates which had been held shut by the river's current. This attack ended the reign of Belshazzar.

WHY is this *children's* tale so important? It proves the author of the book of Daniel was actually there when Babylon fell. Was Daniel wrong? Was this story just made up? Why does Daniel get the name of the last king of the Babylonian empire wrong?   This has been the thinking of the scholars who wanted to date the book of Daniel as being written long after these, and other, events took place.

In 1854, archeological excavations in Mesopotamia discovered the stele of Nabonidus and several small clay cylinders inscribed with accounts of the rebuilding of Ur's ziggurat (temple tower) by King Nabonidus. The inscriptions concluded with prayers for Nabonidus' health—and for his eldest son and co-regent, *Belshazzar!* Additional archeological finds have added details to this amazing reference to Belshazzar. It seems that Nabonidus was not well liked by his subjects. At one point in his reign, he decided to turn over the throne to his son Belshazzar to serve as regent in his place.

Here we see the beauty of the God's ability to preserve His written word accurately. It is clear now, from the archeological record that a writer of 200 BC would not have known that the last king of Babylon was not Nabonidus, but his son and co-regent Belshazzar. Daniel, writing at the time of these events knew the co-regent, Belshazzar personally. God provides us with proof that Daniel was the writer and was writing at the time of these historical events. Look once again at Belshazzar's offer:

> "Whoever reads this writing, and shows me its interpretation, shall be clothed with purple and have a chain of gold around his neck and shall be the third ruler in the kingdom."

Did you see it? Belshazzar was prepared to give almost anything to have the message translated. Did you notice that he offered to promote the person who could translate the message to a position of greatness? But why would he offer to promote that person to be the third highest ruler in the kingdom? It was because Belshazzar knew that he was serving as regent in his father's place. So, Belshazzar was *not* the highest ruler of the land, only the *second* highest ruler. The highest office to which he could elevate an advisor was to serve as the **third** highest ruler of the land. With the discoveries of the 1850's, archeology has found that the Bible accurately presents the history of this event. By the way, archeologists have also found artifacts, from this time period, confirming Daniel's appointment as the third highest ruler of Babylon.

So, we see that a Bible story which we have read and which has been told over and over to children contains the very key to proving its accuracy and authority – naming Daniel to serve as the *third highest ruler* of the kingdom. Such treasures of truth reside throughout this love letter from our Father in heaven to us. We can absolutely depend on its truth and accuracy.

Prayer: Father help me to read Your Word with the same wisdom that Daniel had. Help me to accurately understand Your Truth and apply it to my daily life. May I always read Your Word, knowing that You are communicating Your trustworthiness to me.

REFERENCES

Daniel Interpreting the Handwriting on the Wall. Retrieved from Image Gallery of Christian Theological Seminary http://www.cts.edu/ImageLibrary/Isa_Mal.cfm.
Does Archeology Support the Bible? Retrieved from http://www.myfortress.org/archaeology.htm.
Missler, Chuck. The First Cryptanalyst. Retrieved from http://www.khouse.org/articles/1998/149/

LESSON 5 NOTES:

LESSON 6 – **Why Did Cyrus Send the Jews Home?**

Definition

Prophecy: A prophecy is not a prediction of the future - it is a promise about the future. God gave promises to His prophets. He told them, for example, that the Jews would be forced out of Israel, scattered worldwide, persecuted worldwide, and that they would eventually return to Israel. All of these promises have been fulfilled.

Culture

The Jews believed that there were special people to whom God revealed His future plans. These individuals were called prophets. Now, it is a very easy thing to say that God talked to you and told you to say this or that. To protect His people from false prophets, God established very clear rules regarding prophets and their prophecies:

> "If a prophet or a dreamer of dreams arises among you and gives you a sign or a wonder, and the sign or wonder that he tells you comes to pass, and if he says, 'Let us go after other gods,' which you have not known, 'and let us serve them,' you shall not listen to the words of that prophet or that dreamer of dreams."
> Deuteronomy 13:1-3a

Since God is truth and God is the author of history, He is the only true source for knowing future events. If the "prophet" claims to represent any source other than the True God, then the prophet is a false prophet.

> when a prophet speaks in the name of the LORD, if the word does not come to pass or come true, that is a word that the LORD has not spoken; the prophet has spoken it presumptuously. You need not be afraid of him. Deuteronomy 18:22

In this second test, we find that the prophet must be 100% correct 100% of the time. If the prophet makes a prediction and in due course the prediction is not fulfilled—that is, what is predicted does not come to pass, exactly as foretold —then the prophet is judged to be false.

The Jewish leaders made this second test into a practical requirement which is held consistently throughout the Bible. Before someone could claim to be a prophet of future events, they must include a prophecy which would occur within the life of those hearing the prophecy. This short term prophecy would serve as proof of the truth of the long term prophecy.

The Story of Cyrus

When we consider prophecy, we must always remember that it is God giving us a glimpse of His promise of what is to come, and that the glimpse we get is given to us for a purpose. One of the most specific purposes of prophecy is to demonstrate God's love and care for His people and His trustworthiness in His dealings with men.   What happens in history is not just chance, but is in accordance with God's plan, created before time began.

Remember the first study in this book. We find that as early as the fifth chapter of the Book of Genesis, God has clearly defined His plan for salvation. In the ten names of the genealogy, God's plan is clearly explained.   In the same way, God uses prophecy to demonstrate to us that He is in control of all events. He is indeed sovereign over His creation. God even uses His own prophecies to direct history.

Let's look at a specific example of this use of prophecy.

> ISAIAH 45:1-7 " Thus says the LORD to his anointed, to Cyrus, whose right hand I have grasped, to subdue nations before him and to loose the belts of kings, to open doors before him that gates may not be closed: "I will go before you and level the exalted places, I will break in pieces the doors of bronze and cut through the bars of iron, I will give you the treasures of darkness and the hoards in secret places, that you may know that it is I, the LORD, the God of Israel, who call you by your name.   For the sake of my servant Jacob, and Israel my chosen, I call you by your name, I name you, though you do not know me.   I am the LORD, and there is no other, besides me there is no God; I equip you, though you do not know me, that people may know, from the rising of the sun and from the west, that there is none besides me; I am the LORD, and there is no other. I form light and create darkness, I make well-being and create calamity, I am the LORD, who does all these things."

Isaiah wrote this passage 300 years after the rule of King David and almost 200 years before the fall of Babylon to the Medes and Persians. In his book of prophecies, we find this very interesting passage regarding God's use of a non-believer to restore Jerusalem and to rebuild His Temple there. So, does Isaiah make it as a prophet? Did this specific prediction come true?

Let's look at the fall of Babylon in 539 BC. How was Cyrus able to take this impregnable city? Here is what we know about this ancient city, built 2,500 years ago:

- It was built on (straddling) the Euphrates River;
- The walls were 14 miles long on each side (14 x 14 square), making an enclosure of 196 square miles (Washington, DC is only 68.3 Square miles) ;
- Nebuchadnezzar built a moat 30 feet deep around the city;
- The city had 2 walls and in some places 3 walls, 100 feet wide and over 300 feet tall;
- The walls had over 100 gates made of bronze (fireproof) and secured with iron bars;
- The walls had 250 watch towers 100 feet taller than the walls;

Replica of the Ishtar Gate

- There was enough farmland (and water) to continuously feed the city's inhabitants.

Clearly this city was not to be taken by siege. The one weakness to such a defense would be the places where the Euphrates River entered and exited the city. Nebuchadnezzar II designed two sets of gates where the pressure of the water caused the leaves of the gate to be held tightly against one another. While the river was flowing absolutely no attacker could open the gates. Remember Isaiah's claim that for Cyrus, God would *"open before him the two leaved gates; and the gates shall not be shut?"* (KJV)

The force of the waters of the Euphrates made these gates impregnable. When Cyrus marched up to these magnificent walls of Babylon he was well aware that conventional warfare was never going to take the city; but, Cyrus was knowledgeable of a queen of Babylon called Nitocris.

Nitocris engineered a system to prevent flooding in Babylon. She brought all her men (slaves) to dig out a lake basin 47 miles in circumference. When the Euphrates was about to flood, they diverted some of the river's flow into this reservoir.

Having discovered this reservoir with its diversion canal, Cyrus placed two small detachments of the Persian army observing the city. With the bulk of his forces, Cyrus marched north to look for the reservoir. He found it, cleared it out and prepared to divert the river into the lake basin again. It took him about a year to complete this project.

When it was done he diverted the Euphrates into the lake basin. He then marched the rest of his army back to Babylon. By the time he got there, the river level had fallen dramatically. The flow of the river was no longer strong enough to hold the two river gates closed. When Cyrus arrived, his forces pushed open the gates and marched into the center of the city. This was the same night we read about in Daniel 5! Cyrus took the greatest city in the world, that night, fulfilling a number of prophecies.

But now, we must ask the question **why**? Why would God go to the trouble of having an obscure Jewish prophet 700 years before the birth of the Messiah spend time talking about a pagan ruler to come 200 years in the future? God knew that the Jewish nation would not honor His law and would follow false gods. He knew that to punish them for this sinfulness, He would send them into exile and their cities and the Temple would be utterly destroyed. But God is a God of compassion and He also knew that they would repent and call out to Him from their exile.

God had a plan for the salvation of His entire creation. This plan, as spelled out throughout the Bible, calls for God to send a *kinsman redeemer* for mankind. This redeemer would be God in the flesh, who would die for the sins of the world. But this redeemer would also be a conquering ruler who would restore the law and the proper worship of God. Throughout the history of Israel, God would send a type of the *Kinsman Redeemer* to save the nation from its distress. Cyrus, a gentile, serves as the *Kinsman Redeemer*, now.

What happened in the days after the fall of Babylon? According to the ancient historian, Flavius Josephus, in his work *Antiquities* XI.i.2,

> This was known to Cyrus by his reading the book which Isaiah left behind him of his prophecies; for this prophet said that God had spoken thus to him in a secret vision: "My will is, that Cyrus, whom I have appointed to be king over many and great nations, send back my people to their own land, and build my temple." This was foretold by Isaiah one hundred and forty years before the temple was demolished. Accordingly, when Cyrus read this, and admired the Divine power, an earnest desire and ambition seized upon him to fulfill what was so written; so he called for the most eminent Jews that were in Babylon, and said to them, that he gave them leave to go back to their own country, and to rebuild their city Jerusalem, (2) and the temple of God, for that he would be their assistant, and that he would write to the rulers and governors that were in the neighborhood of their country of Judea, that they should contribute to them gold and silver for the building of the temple, and besides that, beasts for their sacrifices.

Why was Cyrus reading the writings of an obscure Jewish prophet and how did Cyrus come to find himself referenced in the Jew's sacred writings? Who would have been around to give Cyrus a copy of the Book of Isaiah? The night before, Daniel told Belshazzar that he had been weighed and found wanting. For his services, Daniel was elevated to the *Third Highest Ruler* of the kingdom. Overnight, the kingdom had been taken from Belshazzar and according to Daniel, Belshazzar was killed. It is logical to believe that Daniel, based on his new rank, appeared before Cyrus shortly after Cyrus took the city.

Let's recreate the scene. In most cases, the top rulers of a conquered nation were put to death. The more junior officials were spared to keep the government working. Belshazzar, is dead. Daniel appears before Cyrus, seeking an audience or in response to a summons. Cyrus receives him, expecting Daniel to beg for his own life. Daniel, however, has his own agenda. He is appearing before Cyrus, not as Belshazzar's advisor, but as the ambassador for the One True God!

When an ambassador first arrives in the country to which he has been dispatched, he presents his credentials – documents demonstrating the ambassador's authority. In his hands, I believe, Daniel held *his* credentials, the personal letter addressed to Cyrus which has been waiting over 200 years for delivery. It is obvious the impact this encounter had on Cyrus! We see in Ezra 1:

> EZRA 1:1-4 In the first year of Cyrus king of Persia, that the word of the LORD by the mouth of Jeremiah might be fulfilled, the LORD stirred up the spirit of Cyrus king of Persia, so that he made a proclamation throughout all his kingdom and also put it in writing: "Thus says Cyrus king of Persia: The LORD, the God of heaven, has

given me all the kingdoms of the earth, and he has charged me to build him a house at Jerusalem, which is in Judah. Whoever is among you of all his people, may his God be with him, and let him go up to Jerusalem, which is in Judah, and rebuild the house of the LORD, the God of Israel--he is the God who is in Jerusalem. And let each survivor, in whatever place he sojourns, be assisted by the men of his place with silver and gold, with goods and with beasts, besides freewill offerings for the house of God that is in Jerusalem."

Cyrus, a non-believer was moved to issue royal orders, returning the Jews to Israel and rebuilding of the Temple. He also restored all of the Temple treasures which had been taken from Jerusalem by Nebuchadnezzar. These orders from Cyrus ended the Babylonian exile 70 years after its start - the precise span of time predicted by Isaiah.

So Cyrus was used by God to accomplish exactly what He planned. But what about Daniel, the old man who had served as God's Ambassador for so many years? He continued to serve, providing Cyrus with insight from the One True God. Look at these two verses from the book of Daniel:

Daniel 6:28 So this Daniel prospered during the reign of Darius and the reign of Cyrus the Persian.

Daniel 10:1 In the *third year of Cyrus* king of Persia a word was revealed to Daniel, who was named Belteshazzar. And the word was true, and it was a great conflict. And he understood the word and had understanding of the vision.

We see from these verses that Daniel continued to serve under Cyrus. And it was during this time that God sent to Daniel, who had faithfully served these great gentile nations, the vision of the progression of the nations to the end of history.

Prayer: Thank you Father that history is really Your story. Thank you for providing us with stories which show Your love and care for us. Thank you for the faithful service of Your ambassadors, like Daniel. Thank you that we can rest assured that the course of history will be as You have described it in Your Word.

REFERENCES

Josephus, Flavious. *Antiquities.*
Josephus, Flavious. *The Punic Wars.*
Missler, Chuck. *The First Cryptanalyst.* Retrieved from
    http://www.khouse.org/articles/1998/149/.

LESSON 6 NOTES:

LESSON 7 – **Why Did God Use a Witch?**

Definition

Medium: A Medium is a person that is said to communicate with the deceased. Mediumship is the process whereby a human, known as a medium, is used by a spirit or deceased person for the purpose of presenting information. Basically mediumship involves a cooperating effort between a person on Earth and a deceased person - in other words, the ability to communicate with the departed.

Culture

In the Bible, we learn that God created beings we call angels. At one point there was a war in heaven and 1/3 of the angels followed a super angel named Lucifer in rebelling against God. We refer to them as Satan and his demons. When defeated, they were cast down to earth. The Bible tells us that both angels and demons can observe us and can even have interaction with humans on a limited basis.

Throughout history, there have been people, called mediums, who have claimed that they could communicate with the spirits of people who have died. These spirits of the dead are supposed to be able to tell the living things about the future and things unknown. In many cases, these mediums have been shown to be fakes, but there have been some mediums that have had the ability to accurately predict future events or to reveal hidden information in this manner.

God's word clearly teaches that the dead do not communicate with the living. To whom are these mediums speaking? They are communicating with spiritual beings (demons) who are pretending to be the spirits of the dead. If people are depending on mediums to tell them what will happen, they don't see as great a need for God. Turning people away from trusting God is one of the greatest objectives of Satan. This is why demons would impersonate the dead.

Consider this passage:

Saul and the Spirit Medium

I Samuel 28:5-19 When Saul saw the army of the Philistines, he was afraid, and his heart trembled greatly. And when Saul inquired of the LORD, the LORD did not answer him, either by dreams, or by Urim, or by prophets. Then Saul said to his servants, "Seek out for me a woman who is a medium, that I may go to her and inquire of her." And his servants said to him, "Behold, there is a medium at En-dor." So Saul disguised himself and put on other garments and went, he and two men with him. And they came to the woman by night. And he said, "Divine for me by a spirit and bring up for me whomever I shall name to you."

The woman said to him, "Surely you know what Saul has done, how he has cut off the mediums and the necromancers from the land. Why then are you laying a trap for my life to bring about my death?" But Saul swore to her by the LORD, "As the LORD lives, no punishment shall come upon you for this thing." Then the woman said, "Whom shall I bring up for you?" He said, "Bring up Samuel for me." When the woman saw

Samuel, she cried out with a loud voice. And the woman said to Saul, "Why have you deceived me? You are Saul."

The king said to her, "Do not be afraid. What do you see?" And the woman said to Saul, "I see a god coming up out of the earth." He said to her, "What is his appearance?" And she said, "An old man is coming up, and he is wrapped in a robe." And Saul knew that it was Samuel, and he bowed with his face to the ground and paid homage. Then Samuel said to Saul, "Why have you disturbed me by bringing me up?" Saul answered, "I am in great distress, for the Philistines are warring against me, and God has turned away from me and answers me no more, either by prophets or by dreams. Therefore I have summoned you to tell me what I shall do."

And Samuel said, "Why then do you ask me, since the LORD has turned from you and become your enemy? The LORD has done to you as he spoke by me, for the LORD has torn the kingdom out of your hand and given it to your neighbor, David. Because you did not obey the voice of the LORD and did not carry out his fierce wrath against Amalek, therefore the LORD has done this thing to you this day. Moreover, the LORD will give Israel also with you into the hand of the Philistines, and tomorrow you and your sons shall be with me. The LORD will give the army of Israel also into the hand of the Philistines."

The king of Israel is seeking a medium to learn the future. God is no longer communicating with Saul. Let's remember how Saul got to this point of his reign. Saul was anointed by Samuel after the people of Israel had asked God to give them a king (I Samuel 8:1-22).

Saul was from the tribe of Benjamin and a great specimen of a man. He stood a full head taller than other Israelites and had great strength. He delivered his country from the Philistines. The problem with Saul is that his power went to his head. He chose not to follow God's directions and failed to obey God's commands. As Saul's reign progressed, Samuel was told by God to anoint David to replace Saul as king. As we read our story, Samuel, the Judge and Prophet, is dead and God has stopped communicating with Saul. He is truly out of touch for his role as the head of God's chosen people.

Saul is now facing a battle with the Philistines. He can stand the silence no longer. He breaks God's and his own law seeking the services of a medium. In Leviticus 19:31 we read *"Do not turn to mediums or seek out spiritists, for you will be defiled by them. I am the LORD your God."* Because of this law, Saul had expelled all of the mediums and spiritualist from the land early in his reign. But now, we find that spiritualism has crept back into the nation of Israel. Notice that Saul's advisors knew where to find a medium, even though this practice was forbidden. Saul breaks God's law and his own ordinance with a quick trip to Endor.

Saul disguises himself and tells her that he wants her to call up someone who has died. She refuses saying to do so, she could be put to death. Saul assures her that he can protect her from any punishment.

At this point we have to ask "who did the witch think this visitor was?" Who could protect her from the king's ordinance? Does she know it is Saul? I don't thinks so – at least not yet. Notice how Saul swears by the LORD that the witch will not die. How often do we wrap sinful acts in the righteousness of God's name?

Saul is successful in convincing the witch to use her powers. Look carefully at the text. The witch would actually deceive her clients by calling on a familiar spirit. This spirit (or demon) would then imitate the dead person that the client was seeking. Now, having been convinced by Saul that she will be protected from punishment, she seeks to contact her familiar spirit. But to her surprise and fear, it is not her familiar that comes up – *it is Samuel!*

Notice that everyone is absolutely convinced that Samuel has really appeared from the dead. This fact is not only unquestioned, it is verified by the terror of the medium who is totally out of her normal operation, working through familiar spirits.

Why did God include this event in the Bible? What is God's purpose for this story and what truth are we to take from it to apply to our lives. Actually, I would pose another question which should shed light on what we seek to learn. Where did Saul go after he died? Saul was chosen by God to be king over His people. Saul failed to measure up to God's commandments. God could no longer depend on Saul to lead Israel. God withdrew the covering of His Spirit and passed it to David. So, did Saul *lose his salvation*? For failing to obey God, did Saul get condemned to spend eternity separated from God? More plainly stated, *did Saul **fall from grace***?

In revealing the next day's events, Samuel tells Saul "tomorrow you and your sons will be with me". The choice of words here is key. There are many ways that Samuel could have expressed Saul's death. We know from the story Jesus told of Lazarus and Davies that the place for the dead was divided into two realms with an uncrossable gulf in between. We find this in Luke:

> LUKE 16:19-31 "There was a rich man who was clothed in purple and fine linen and who feasted sumptuously every day. And at his gate was laid a poor man named Lazarus, covered with sores, the rich man's table. Moreover, even the dogs came and licked his sores. The poor man died and was carried by the angels to Abraham's side. The rich man also died and was buried, and in Hades, being in torment, he lifted up his eyes and saw Abraham far off and Lazarus at his side. And he called out, 'Father Abraham, have mercy on me, and send Lazarus to dip the end of his finger in water and cool my tongue, for I am in anguish in this flame.' But Abraham said, 'Child, remember that you in your lifetime received your good things, and Lazarus in like manner bad things; but now he is comforted here, and you are in anguish. And besides all this, between us and you a great chasm has been fixed, in order that those who would pass from here to you may not be able, and none may cross from there to us.' And he said, 'Then I beg you, father, to send him to my father's house-- for I have five brothers--so that he may warn them, lest they also come into this place of torment.' But Abraham said, 'They have Moses and the Prophets; let them hear them.' And he said, 'No, father Abraham, but if someone goes to them from the dead, they will repent.' He said to him, 'If they do not hear Moses and the Prophets, neither will they be convinced if someone should rise from the dead.'"

Abraham himself tells the rich man that there is no crossing between the two realms. Jesus tells this to His disciples as fact. Whenever He tells parables, he does not use proper names. When he reveals true stories He uses people's names. Since we know the names in this story, we know this story is not a parable but revealed truth.

Let's apply what Christ describes to Samuel's message given to Saul. Saul and his sons will be with Samuel when they die, tomorrow. And there is no doubt that Samuel is on the side of the gulf with Abraham. This side is referred to as the *bosom of Abraham*. So, from Samuel's appearance, we can answer the question of Saul's resting place. He and his sons reside with Abraham.

Abraham's faith was accounted as righteousness and he waits, with all of the saints who have died, for the final day of resurrection. Now we can see that Saul and his sons will be in this group as well.

So why did God give us this story? One of the controversial teachings of some denominations of the Christian faith is the *Perseverance of the Saints*. This is the belief that once a person comes to a saving faith in Christ, there is nothing that person can do to lose his or her ultimate salvation. With Saul, we see him falling away from his relationship with God. When God permitted Samuel to come up from the dead, Samuel confirmed that Saul and his sons would end up in the B*osom of Abraham*.

This passage is about Saul's ultimate act of rebellion against God. By seeking the counsel of a medium, Saul shows us someone who has known God's love and protection and then, *for a while fallen into grievous sin.* If anyone should have lost his salvation, surely it would have been Saul! Yet, as Samuel tells us, Saul rests in the *bosom of Abraham* and will ultimately dwell and reign in heaven.

Prayer: Thank you, Father, for the assurance of effectual calling on our lives. We have the confidence that once we are covered by Your Son's shed blood our ultimate dwelling place is in Your presence. May our time on earth be marked by our steady growth to become more like Christ and may we never choose grievous sin over walking in Your glorious light!

REFERENCES

Gerten-Jackson, Carol. 1996. The Witch of Endor. Carol Jenson Fine Art. Retrieved from http://cgfa.sunsite.dk/mount/p-mount2.htm.

LESSON 7 NOTES:

LESSON 8 – Why Did Jesus Go Late to the Feast of the Tabernacles Celebration?

Definition

Epiphany means a manifestation, usually of divine power. Thus the actual appearance of God (as in the burning bush) or a moment of divine revelation may be called an epiphany.

Culture

Within the cycle of rituals in the year, Jewish men were expected to appear at the Temple at three specific festivals: Passover, Pentecost, and Tabernacles. In general, the duty of *appearing before the Lord* at the services of His house was considered to be mandatory. Here an important rabbinical principle came into play. Although not expressed in Scripture, this principle seems clearly founded upon it - 'a sacrifice could not be offered for any one unless he himself were present,' to present and to lay his hand upon it (Leviticus 1:3, 3:2, 3:8). [Edersheim] Clearly, the need for a sacrificial covering for sin is an individual need.

Christ Proclaims His Mission

JOHN 7:37-43 On the last day of the feast, the great day, Jesus stood up and cried out, "If anyone thirsts, let him come to me and drink. Whoever believes in me, as the Scripture has said, 'Out of his heart will flow rivers of living water.'" Now this he said about the Spirit, whom those who believed in him were to receive, for as yet the Spirit had not been given, because Jesus was not yet glorified. When they heard these words, some of the people said, "This really is the Prophet." Others said, "This is the Christ." But some said, "Is the Christ to come from Galilee? Has not the Scripture said that the Christ comes from the offspring of David, and comes from Bethlehem, the village where David was?" So there was a division among the people over him.

The feast in this passage is the Jewish Feast of Tabernacles (or Booths) approximately 6 months before Jesus' crucifixion. To understand the depth of meaning in the words spoken by Jesus, it is necessary to first understand this feast and the rituals which were being performed.

This festival was the most joyous one of the year. It celebrated the successful harvest and storing of the crops and fruits. The work of the year was completed and the nation was looking forward to the winter rains which would prepare the earth for the next year's crops.

It was also at this time each year that the Jewish nation was called to look back on the time they spent in the Wilderness (living in booths) and to look forward to the final harvest and the completion of Israel's historical mission – the ingathering of all nations to worship the Lord.

Consider the passage from Zechariah 14:16-17, 21b:

Then everyone who survives of all the nations that have come against Jerusalem shall go up year after year to worship the King, the LORD of hosts, and to keep the Feast of Booths. And if any of the families of the earth do not go up to Jerusalem to worship the King, the LORD of hosts, there will be no rain on them.... And there shall no longer be a trader in the house of the LORD of hosts on that day.

The pressing question is **why**, after coming secretly into Jerusalem (John 7:10), did Jesus chose to make His public announcement on the last day of the Festival (John 7:37-38). Let's see what was happening in the Temple on this day.

The festivities of the Week of Tabernacles are drawing to a close. It is the last day, the 'Day of the Great Hosanna,' when the worshippers march seven times around the altar and shout 'Hosanna'. On this particular day, the priest returns from the pool of Siloam. For the last time, he pours the contents of his pitcher into a funnel on the altar. The water flows down and comes out on the floor of the Temple in an image of the heavenly temple seen in Ezekiel 47:1-2.

After the 'Hallel' is sung to the sound of the flute, the priests blow three blasts from their silver trumpets. As the last words of Psalm 118 fade and the interest of the people is raised to its highest pitch, a single voice is raised from amidst the mass of worshippers. It echoes through the Temple; startling the crowd; and triggers fear and hatred in the hearts of the Temple leadership. It is Jesus, who stands and cries, 'if any man thirst let him come unto Me, and drink.' Then by faith in Him should each one truly become like the Pool of Siloam, and from his inmost being 'rivers of living waters flow' (John 7:38).

Why does Jesus chose to speak out now? Understanding the meaning of the Festival of the Tabernacles, we can appreciate what is really going on. The true significance of the ceremony in which the worshipers have just taken part, is not only fully explained by Jesus, but the manner of its fulfillment is pointed out. Can you remember some point in your life when the rituals of worship suddenly came to life for you?   A time when your understanding suddenly caught up? A point where the meaning of an act of worship suddenly became tangible? You call such a moment an epiphany.

On this day, in the Temple, the effect of the epiphany (Jesus' revelation) was instantaneous.   The vast assembly responded when brought face to face with 'Him in whom every type and prophecy is fulfilled'. There were many who, 'when they heard this saying, said, of a truth this is the Prophet. Others said, this is the Christ.'

Even the Temple guard, whose duty it was to arrest anyone who interrupted the services of the day 'dared not to lay hands on Him.' 'Never man spake like this man,' was the only account they could give in answer to the reproaches of the chief priests and Pharisees.

The rebuke of the Jewish authorities followed. They plotted to put Jesus to death. Nicodemus alone seemed moved by Jesus' clear declaration of himself as the Messiah. Remember that it was Nicodemus who visited Jesus under the cover of darkness. Now, he cautions the Sanhedrin from acting against Christ, He does so in the genuine rabbinical manner of argument. Instead of challenging the court directly, Nicodemus asked the question: 'Doth our law judge any man before it hear him, and know what he doeth?'

What does this episode teach us about God's purpose? Let's start with the establishment of the Festivals of Tabernacles. It is easy to view this festival as a reminder of God's intervention in the past – the completed harvest, the completed year, or the exodus from Egypt. But God placed another purpose in the rituals. He placed a code for revealing the Redeemer of Israel. As the water flowed forth from the altar, so would the rivers of living water flow forth from God in the Flesh. God placed this information in His festival so that in the fullness of time the Chosen One would stand up in that place and be seen for who he is.

Think about this. When Solomon dedicated the Temple, the Shekinah glory of God entered and indwelled the Holy of Holies. Since the Temple was rebuilt by Cyrus, God's glory never returned to the Holy of Holies. The Ark of the Covenant had disappeared before the exile to Babylon and never returned to the Holy of Holies. Now, hundreds of years later, God returned to the Temple. Only, this time, His glory was hidden in the form of a man. As Jesus entered the Temple, it was not to be confined behind the veil that blocked the Holy of Holies, but to stand in the midst of the people and to be revealed. On this special day, described to us by the Beloved Disciple, Jesus used the rituals established by God to declare God's love and desire for man's redemption and restoration to fellowship. On this day, many of the Jews experienced the epiphany. Now that we understand the ritual as well, we can join in the understanding and marvel at God's purpose.

Prayer: Thank you, Father, that you use so many different ways to tell us we can trust you. Even in rituals thousands of years old, you have placed Your truths for us to find. Give us a questioning mind as we seek to grow in our knowledge of You. Let your living waters flow from us so that those around us have an opportunity to drink and be satisfied.

REFERENCE

Edersheim, Alfred. 1874. The Temple- Its Ministry and Service. E-Sword 7.7.0. Retrieved from http://www.e-sword.com.

LESSON 8 NOTES:

LESSON 9 – **Why Did Jesus Tarry?**

Definition

Tarry - to remain or stay, as in a place; sojourn; to delay or be tardy in acting, starting, coming, etc.; linger or loiter.

Culture

The Jewish people traveled to Jerusalem three times a year for the High Feasts. Obviously, this influx of visitors taxed the city's housing resources. Many of the visitors would stay in the surrounding countryside – caves being prize locations. Unfortunately, many caves were used as tombs. If a Jew should enter one it would defile him and make him ineligible to participate in the feast and religious observances. For this reason, Jews took care to have their tombs white-washed each year, that, being easily discovered, they might consequently be avoided.

Jesus Raises Lazarus

> **John 11:1-6,11-15, 17,20-27, 32-46, 53** Now a certain man was ill, Lazarus of Bethany, the village of Mary and her sister Martha. It was Mary who anointed the Lord with ointment and wiped his feet with her hair, whose brother Lazarus was ill. So the sisters sent to him, saying, "Lord, he whom you love is ill."
>
> But when Jesus heard it he said, "This illness does not lead to death. It is for the glory of God, so that the Son of God may be glorified through it." Now Jesus loved

Martha and her sister and Lazarus. So, when he heard that Lazarus was ill, he stayed two days longer in the place where he was.

After saying these things, he said to them, "Our friend Lazarus has fallen asleep, but I go to awaken him." The disciples said to him, "Lord, if he has fallen asleep, he will recover." Now Jesus had spoken of his death, but they thought that he meant taking rest in sleep. Then Jesus told them plainly, "Lazarus has died, and for your sake I am glad that I was not there, so that you may believe. But let us go to him."

Now when Jesus came, he found that Lazarus had already been in the tomb four days…. So when Martha heard that Jesus was coming, she went and met him, but Mary remained seated in the house. Martha said to Jesus, "Lord, if you had been here, my brother would not have died. But even now I know that whatever you ask from God, God will give you." Jesus said to her, "Your brother will rise again." Martha said to him, "I know that he will rise again in the resurrection on the last day." Jesus said to her, "I am the resurrection and the life. Whoever believes in me, though he die, yet shall he live, and everyone who lives and believes in me shall never die. Do you believe this?" She said to him, "Yes, Lord; I believe that you are the Christ, the Son of God, who is coming into the world."

Now when Mary came to where Jesus was and saw him, she fell at his feet, saying to him, "Lord, if you had been here, my brother would not have died." When Jesus saw her weeping, and the Jews who had come with her also weeping, he was deeply moved in his spirit and greatly troubled. And he said, "Where have you laid him?" They said to him, "Lord, come and see." Jesus wept.

So the Jews said, "See how he loved him!" But some of them said, "Could not he who opened the eyes of the blind man also have kept this man from dying?" Then Jesus, deeply moved again, came to the tomb. It was a cave, and a stone lay against it. Jesus said, "Take away the stone." Martha, the sister of the dead man, said to him, "Lord, by this time there will be an odor, for he has been dead four days." Jesus said to her, "Did I not tell you that if you believed you would see the glory of God?"

So they took away the stone. And Jesus lifted up his eyes and said, "Father, I thank you that you have heard me. I knew that you always hear me, but I said this on account of the people standing around, that they may believe that you sent me." When he had said these things, he cried out with a loud voice, "Lazarus, come out." The man who had died came out, his hands and feet bound with linen strips, and his face wrapped with a cloth. Jesus said to them, "Unbind him, and let him go."

Many of the Jews therefore, who had come with Mary and had seen what he did, believed in him, but some of them went to the Pharisees and told them what Jesus had done.

So from that day on they [the Council] made plans to put him to death.

This is a passage that is recorded only by John. It illustrates what he believes to be the catalyst to the events resulting in Jesus' crucifixion and ultimately His own resurrection from the dead.

Jesus has raised the dead two times before the resurrection of Lazarus. In Luke 7:11-17, Jesus restores life to a widow's son. A second raising of the dead appears in all three of the synoptic Gospels (Matthew, Mark, and Luke) – the raising of Jairus' daughter. Jesus tells Jairus that his daughter is not dead, only asleep. When He arrives at Jairus' home, Jesus does indeed return her to the realm of the living.

When He raised the widow's son, fear seized the people of the region, and they glorified God. Similarly, people were amazed to see such a miracle when Jesus raised Jairus' daughter from the dead. Jesus even used these instances to reassure John the Baptist that He was the Messiah:

> Luke 7:20-23 And when the men had come to him, they said, "John the Baptist has sent us to you, saying, 'Are you the one who is to come, or shall we look for another?'" In that hour he healed many people of diseases and plagues and evil spirits, and on many who were blind he bestowed sight. And he answered them, "Go and tell John what you have seen and heard: the blind receive their sight, the lame walk, lepers are cleansed, and the deaf hear, *the dead are raised up*, the poor have good news preached to them. And blessed is the one who is not offended by me."

When Jesus raised Lazarus from the dead, what was the response from the observers?

> John 11:47-48, 53 So the chief priests and the Pharisees gathered the Council and said, "What are we to do? For this man performs many signs. If we let him go on like this, everyone will believe in him, and the Romans will

come and take away both our place and our nation." So from that day on they made plans to put him to death.

Why did the raising of Lazarus bring this type of response? Jesus has restored two others to life, so why should the resurrection of Lazarus cause such a different response? The answer to this question can be found with a little bit of investigation.

As the story of Lazarus begins, Jesus is some distance from Bethany. A messenger arrives from Mary and Martha saying that Lazarus is ill. Look at John's detail. He informs us that Jesus loved Mary, Martha, and Lazarus! The next statement then says, "So, He stayed two more days" where He was. Then Jesus and His disciples travel to Bethany, arriving four days after Lazarus' death. From this timetable, we can see that it took Jesus two days to travel to Bethany. With Lazarus, dead for four days and Jesus tarrying two days, we can see that Lazarus was dead when the messenger arrived to tell Jesus that he was ill!

Stop and consider the implication of this fact. If Jesus had not tarried, but traveled to Bethany immediately, Lazarus would have been two days in the tomb – in either case, Jesus knew that He would resurrect Lazarus – "This illness does not lead to death. It is for the glory of God, so that the Son of God may be glorified through it."(v4)

How was Jesus received by Mary and Martha? Martha met Jesus before He even arrived at Bethany. Her response to Jesus was "Lord, if you had been here, my brother would not have died. " (v21). When Jesus told her that Lazarus would rise again, she responded, "I know that he will rise again in the resurrection on the *last day*." Mary's response was similar. She said, "Lord, if you had been here, my brother would not have died."

Both these women had been closely associated with Jesus, His disciples, and His ministry. There is no way that they did not know of the other events where Jesus brought the dead back to life. Yet, here they act as if they do not know of these events - they don't even ask if it might be possible for Jesus to raise their brother.

If a loved one had died and I knew someone who could raise people from the dead, I know I would at least ask that person to try to resurrect my loved one. **Why** did Martha and Mary not ask Jesus to try?

Let's start by understanding how people viewed death back then. At the time of Christ, people believed that the spirit of the dead would hover around the body, trying to rejoin it in life, until corruption set in. Once the body experienced corruption, the spirit of the deceased would depart. How long was this time until corruption? Three days!

Check out this verse and pay attention to the number of days mentioned -

> Numbers 19:11-12 "Whoever touches the dead body of any person shall be unclean seven days. He shall cleanse himself with the water on the third day and on the seventh day, and so be clean. But if he does not cleanse himself on the third day and on the seventh day, he will not become clean."

Notice the requirement to be cleansed at day three.

> **Hosea 6:1-2** "Come, let us return to the LORD; for he has torn us, that he may heal us; he has struck us down, and he will bind us up. After two days he will

revive us; on the third day he will raise us up, that we may live before him.

Again, the raising up will occur on the third day after death. In his work, *The Life and Time of Jesus the Messiah*, Edersheim points out that the relatives and friends of the deceased would visit the grave up to the third day so as to make sure the person was really dead.

King David in Psalm 16:10 says, "For you will not abandon my soul to Sheol, or let your holy one see corruption." Obviously, David was not speaking of himself, but of the Messiah to come. Jesus was in the tomb for only 3 days because, by prophecy, His resurrection had to occur before corruption set in.

Understanding this belief that corruption set in after three days and from that point, the deceased's spirit departed and the dead were considered to be *truly dead*, we see a reason for Jesus' delay.

When Jesus arrived, Lazarus had been dead for 4 days. Remember that even though the messenger told Jesus that Lazarus was ill, Jesus immediately started talking to His disciples about Lazarus and sleep and death. If Jesus had departed for Bethany immediately upon receipt of Mary and Martha's message, He still would have arrived after Lazarus was dead. There was purpose in Jesus' timing.

> John 11:39 Jesus said, "Take away the stone." Martha, the sister of the dead man, said to him, "Lord, by this time there will be an odor, for he has been dead four days."

Because Jesus waited, he arrived after corruption had set in and the spirit of Lazarus would have departed. You see, in the other cases of resurrection, corruption had not set in. So, the observers would have seen Jesus' acts as amazing, but not impossible because the spirits of the dead were still hovering around, trying to get back into their bodies. When Lazarus walked out of the tomb, he was a *living-walking-breathing* example that Jesus had command over life and death!

Here are a couple of interesting notes and observations – first, Jesus calls Lazarus by name. Many scholars say that without specifically identifying Lazarus, Jesus' call to awake would have raised everyone buried in the cemetery.

Second, when Lazarus walks out of the tomb wrapped in his burial linens, all signs of corruption are gone. His body is perfectly restored. When Jesus restores life, it is life in its fullest.

This miracle backed up Jesus' claim to be the Messiah. From this time, the Jewish leaders were out to kill not only Jesus but also Lazarus because Lazarus had become a walking expression of Jesus' power and authority.

> John 12:9-11 When the large crowd of the Jews learned that Jesus was there, they came, not only on account of him but also to see Lazarus, whom he had raised from the dead. So the chief priests made plans to put Lazarus to death as well, because on account of him many of the Jews were going away and believing in Jesus.

One more note from this amazing story. Jesus was in complete control. Remember He said:

> John 10:17-18 For this reason the Father loves me, because I lay down my life that I may take it up again. No one takes it from me, but I lay it down of my own accord. I have authority to lay it down, and I have authority to take it up again. This charge I have received from my Father."

And then in this passage we have another cryptic statement from a surprising source:

> John 11:49-53 But one of them, Caiaphas, who was high priest that year, said to them, "You know nothing at all. Nor do you understand that *it is better for you that one man should die for the people, not that the whole nation should perish.*" He did not say this of his own accord, but being high priest that year he **prophesied** that Jesus would die for the nation, and not for the nation only, but also to gather into one the children of God who are scattered abroad. So from that day on they made plans to put him to death. (Italics mine)

We know that God establishes all of the positions of leadership and authority. Remember Cyrus and how God used him.

Here we have Caiaphas, a man whom God has placed in the office of High Priest. God has given him a vision, and he has spoken it as prophecy. Because the word *prophecy* is used, it tells us that Caiaphas has spoken it prior to this event and has done so within a framework of it being a revelation from God.

God has set the timing, the players, and the events to bring to fulfillment the very plan that He set in motion back in the Garden of Eden. A plan that had Jesus tarry for two days so that there would be no doubt that He was and is the Lord and Giver of Life!

Prayer: It is with thankfulness, Father, that we recognize that You accomplish what You purpose! We trust You to complete the good work You have started in our lives.

REFERENCE

Definition of Tarry retrieved from http://dictionary.reference.com/browse/tarry.
Edersheim, Alfred, *The Life and Times of Jesus the Messiah*, vol.2, 8th edition, Longmans Green, New York, 1896, p.630. In this work Edersheim has listed a number of references from rabbinical sources.
Information on White-washing Tombs retrieved from http://www.sacred-texts.com/bib/cmt/clarke/mat023.htm.

LESSON 9 NOTES:

LESSON 10 – Why Did They All Fall Down?

Definition

Judas kiss - an act of seeming friendship that conceals some treachery. When soldiers came to arrest Jesus, Judas identified their victim by kissing him. The next day, driven by guilt, Judas hanged himself.

Culture

What is happening in the Garden while Christ awaits the traitor's arrival?

> Selected Verses from Matthew 26:36-46 Then Jesus went with his disciples to a place called Gethsemane, and he said to them, "Sit here while I go over there and pray." …. Going a little farther, he fell with his face to the ground and prayed, "My Father, if it is possible, may this cup be taken from me. Yet not as I will, but as you will." …. He went away a second time and prayed, "My Father, if it is not possible for this cup to be taken away unless I drink it, may your will be done." …. So he left them and went away once more and prayed the third time, saying the same thing. Then he returned to the disciples and said to them, "Are you still sleeping and resting? Look, the hour is near, and the Son of Man is betrayed into the hands of sinners. Rise, let us go! Here comes my betrayer!"

In Genesis 15, God makes a covenant with Abraham in which God promises to bear the punishment of breaking the covenant should Abraham or any of his descendants break its terms. Here in the

Garden, we see God being true to His word. As Jesus struggles – to the point of sweating blood – with His passion which lies ahead, He asks His Father for release. Why does God, who gives all good things, not honor this request? To permit the cup to pass from Christ, God would have to break His covenant with Abraham to bear the punishment. If God had done so, He would have ceased to be God! So, in the darkness of this night, God the Father has to deny this request of God the Son and turns His back on His Son for the sake of the world. By keeping this covenant, Christ allows God to be the justifier of all covenants.

Christ Proclaims His Deity

> John 18:1-11 When Jesus had spoken these words, he went out with his disciples across the Kidron Valley, where there was a garden, which he and his disciples entered. Now Judas, who betrayed him, also knew the place, for Jesus often met there with his disciples. So Judas, having procured a band of soldiers and some officers from the chief priests and the Pharisees, went there with lanterns and torches and weapons. Then Jesus, knowing all that would happen to him, came forward and said to them, "Whom do you seek?" They answered him, "Jesus of Nazareth." Jesus said to them, "I am he." Judas, who betrayed him, was standing with them. When Jesus said to them, "I am he," they drew back and fell to the ground. So he asked them again, "Whom do you seek?" And they said, "Jesus of Nazareth." Jesus answered, "I told you that I am he. So, if you seek me, let these men go." This was to fulfill the word that he had spoken: "Of those whom you gave me I have lost not one." Then Simon Peter, having a sword, drew it and struck the high priest's servant and cut off his

right ear. (The servant's name was Malchus.) So Jesus said to Peter, "Put your sword into its sheath; shall I not drink the cup that the Father has given me?"

Try to place yourself into this scene. The night is dark; the city is, for the most part, quiet. Jesus and His followers are in the quiet, cool garden. They are exhausted. None of the disciples understand what is about to transpire. Christ has been telling them with increasing frequency that He must go away. But surely, the disciples are not thinking it will be tonight! They have enjoyed the Seder meal. Now, after a short stay in the garden, Jesus rouses them, they think, to continue on to Bethany, as they have done on other nights.

As they assemble, we can see them wiping sleep from their eyes, pulling their cloaks about them, perhaps stretching out a cramped muscle or splashing water on their faces and taking a quick drink from some cool fountain. They gather around Jesus, ready to be off; but He stands there, looking down the path they climbed an hour or two before. What is Jesus waiting for; they might ask one another?

There it is - a light on the pathway from the city. At this point, the disciples are probably anxious to be on their way. Yet, Christ lingers in the garden, watching the steady approach of what now can be seen as torches in the hands of an approaching group of armed men. Do any thoughts stray to Judas and where he might be? Probably not at this moment. As the group approaches, beneath the torches, it is clear from the antique armor worn by the men that these are not Roman legionnaires, but members of the Temple guard. Now, an icy fear grips the disciples. They know of the plots the Jewish leaders have made against Jesus. This armed band represents the might of the Chief Priest and the Pharisees. Surely Jesus will have them scatter and hide. But Jesus simply stands and watches their measured approach.

Now, beneath the glow of the approaching torches, individual members of the band can be picked out. In the lead, walking ahead of the commander of the detachment is a single figure without armor. It is Judas. He *is* leading this armed contingent, through the dark night, right to where Jesus and the disciples wait. Confusion quickly adds to the growing sense of fear. And still Jesus stands and awaits the approaching band. Little do the disciples understand that this moment was one of the great moments in all of history. At this moment the ultimate struggle between good and evil is about to be engaged.

Let's consider the band of men approaching. What Judas offers the High Priest, for money, is the opportunity to seize Jesus when the numbers around Him are the smallest. Without a doubt, Judas reported the number of the group which will be found in the Garden. To subdue a force of twelve, the guard from the Temple would have numbered at least forty (3 to 1 odds) or more men. Tagging along with this armed force come all of the *officials* who would want to be on hand to see *this messianic upstart get what is coming to him.* Look at how Luke reports the event:

> Luke 22:52-53 Then Jesus said to the chief priests, the officers of the temple guard, and the elders, who had come for him, "Am I leading a rebellion, that you have come with swords and clubs? Every day I was with you in the temple courts, and you did not lay a hand on me. But this is your hour - when darkness reigns."

See the large group of observers who are present? These men of *distinction* would not travel without their own body guards, trusted slaves armed with swords and/or clubs. These additional people would have swelled the party from the High Priest to well over 60 – 70 people. Perhaps the throng was close to 100 people. This is the scene with which the tired, frightened disciples are faced, while Jesus just stands there, waiting for the kiss He knows will come from Judas.

Shift to the observations of one who was there. We hear John's words again:

> Then Jesus, knowing all that would happen to him, came forward and said to them, "Whom do you seek?"
>
> They answered him, "Jesus of Nazareth."
>
> Jesus said to them, "I am he." Judas, who betrayed him, was standing with them. When Jesus said to them, "I am he," they drew back and fell to the ground.
>
> So he asked them again, "Whom do you seek?"
>
> And they said, "Jesus of Nazareth."
>
> Jesus answered, "I told you that I am he. So, if you seek me, let these men go."

Here we have a familiar passage of scripture which we have read and reread. Look a little more closely at something very strange:

> John 18:6 ***When Jesus said to them, "I am he," they drew back and fell to the ground.***

Here is the point where we must ask ***why?*** Why did this large contingent of armed guards and powerful men fall to the ground?

What is happening in this garden? What happens immediately prior to the actions of the crowd? Christ states *"I am he"*.

There are numerous scriptures in the Bible where God uses this phrase – among them Isaiah 41:4, 43:10-13, 46:3-4, 48:12-13, Mark 13:4-7, Luke 21:7-9 . And notice this passage in the Gospel of John:

> John 13:17-20 If you know these things, blessed are you if you do them. I am not speaking of all of you; I know whom I have chosen. But the Scripture will be fulfilled, 'He who ate my bread has lifted his heel against me.' I am telling you this now, before it takes place, that when it does take place you may believe that I am he. Truly, truly, I say to you, whoever receives the one I send receives me, and whoever receives me receives the one who sent me."

We see this phrase used repeatedly as an expression defining God. Of course, the most famous passage comes from Exodus. Take a look at this familiar text:

> 3:13-14 Then Moses said to God, "If I come to the people of Israel and say to them, 'The God of your fathers has sent me to you,' and they ask me, 'What is his name?' what shall I say to them?"

> God said to Moses, "*I AM WHO I AM*." And he said, "Say this to the people of Israel, 'I AM has sent me to you.'"

Here I think we begin to find our answer to our question, why. As the Temple force approaches to seize Christ, He chooses to pull back the curtain of His humanity and display His deity. He challenges the force by asking them whom do they seek? The reply comes back "Jesus of Nazareth".

In this moment, Jesus, the Messiah responds, I believe, in the same way that He responded to Moses from the burning bush – "I am He," or as the Old Testament renders it, "*I am who I am*." With this pronouncement, the whole authority of the God of the universe drives the people in the garden to the ground. Recall Isaiah 45:23:

> By myself I have sworn; from my mouth has gone out in righteousness a word that shall not return: 'To me every knee shall bow, every tongue shall swear allegiance.'

As Jesus utters this declaration, the people in the garden cannot help but recognize His authority and thus are driven to the ground. They find themselves "eating dirt". Think of this, all of these people are present for the arrest of Jesus, "the lunatic who has been proclaiming himself to be the Messiah". If my analysis is accurate, they all, once again, hear Him proclaim that He is the Messiah. Jesus declares Himself to be the Messiah, with indisputable certainty, before this crowd itching to arrest him and take him to trial. What other explanation can there be?

Christ declares Himself as the Messiah, so what? It is not like He hasn't done so in many other ways at many other times. In fact, enough people believe Him that the Chief Priest and Pharisees are worried about it. To find an answer to this new question, we once again use the question *why* as our tool for analysis.

Why did Christ disclose his deity in this way? Let's dig a little deeper. Christ and His disciples are surrounded by an armed and angry mob. It has the characteristics of a lynch mob. The synoptic Gospels indicate that the disciples, who have two swords among them, ask Jesus if they should fight. We know from the accounts that Peter actually draws a sword and cuts off the ear of the High Priest's servant.

This action should provoke, if not the Temple guards then, at least the other armed members of the crowd against the disciples. Christ restores Malchus' ear, but even with the marvel of such a miracle, it would be difficult to protect His disciples from harm. Jesus, says as much in the verses, John 18: 8-9:

> Jesus answered, "I told you that I am he. So, if you seek me, let these men go." This was to fulfill the word that he had spoken: "Of those whom you gave me I have lost not one."

By revealing His authority as the Lord of the Universe, Jesus ensures that the disciples are not harmed by this mob.

Were the people of the mob convinced of Christ's Messianic claims? In His trial before Caiaphas, Christ is accused of the crime of blasphemy – that He claimed to be God. To convict Him, there had to be at least two witnesses who testified exactly the same to the crime. The High Priest could not find two witnesses that agreed in their testimony. Now, consider this fact a little more carefully. With all of the people in the garden who were involved with the seizing of Christ, who heard him utter the Messianic claim of "*I am He*", apparently not one of them stands now to testify against Jesus. Despite their allegiance to Caiaphas, they cannot bring themselves to testify against Jesus, because they have heard the voice of God declaring "*I am He*".

Prayer, Thank you, Father, for Your authority and Your purpose. Thank you that I can bow my knee to You now, knowing You as the Lord of the Universe, rather than later when all of those who have ignored You are called to recognize You for who You are. Thank you for the revealing messages in Your written word which show that we can trust You in big things and in small.

LESSON 10 NOTES:

LESSON 11 – **Why Did Jesus Refuse Mary's Embrace?**

Definition

Yom Kippur: The Day of Atonement (lit. covering), is the sixth of the seven Biblical feasts given by God to the nation Israel (Lev. 23:26-32). Observed on the tenth day of the seventh month (Tishrei), it is perhaps the most solemn day on the Jewish calendar. God commanded Israel to observe the Day of Atonement because they were a sinful people in need of cleansing so that they might have continued fellowship with Him.

Culture

Because of the warm climate, the lack of embalming, and the widespread belief that a corpse was ritually unclean, burial or entombment in biblical times was done without delay, usually within 24 hours after death. To die unburied was a horrible fate.

Wealthy people were often placed in tombs outside of towns in family caves or sepulchers cut out of rock. Usually, the bodies were washed, clothed, wrapped in a shroud, sprinkled with aromatic herbs, and laid on a stone platform inside the sepulcher…. Tombs were sealed with a hinged door or a heavy wheel shaped stone.

Fulfillment of the Ritual

> John 20:11-17 But Mary stood weeping outside the tomb, and as she wept she stooped to look into the tomb. And she saw two angels in white, sitting where the body of Jesus had lain, one at the head and one at the feet. They said to her, "Woman, why are you weeping?" She said to them, "They have taken away my Lord, and I do not know where they have laid him." Having said this, she turned around and saw Jesus standing, but she did not know that it was Jesus.
>
> Jesus said to her, "Woman, why are you weeping? Whom are you seeking?" Supposing him to be the gardener, she said to him, "Sir, if you have carried him away, tell me where you have laid him, and I will take him away." Jesus said to her, "Mary." She turned and said to him in Aramaic, "Rabboni!" (which means Teacher). Jesus said to her, "Do not cling to me, for I have not yet ascended to the Father; but go to my brothers and say to them, 'I am ascending to my Father and your Father, to my God and your God.'"

Most of us know this story by heart. We can imagine Mary, saddened and confused, wanting only to know that Jesus has been properly tended to. What joy there must have been when she realizes that Jesus has risen from the dead!

Mary's recognition of Jesus, followed by her dash to embrace Him are soon dampened by His statement – "Do not cling to me"
(The Greek word is *haptomai – to attach oneself).* Most of us accept this statement and continue on our way through the Scriptures. But now we have to ask the question. **Why** was Mary not permitted to embrace Christ at this time?

Christ, in His own explanation states that it is "because I have not yet ascended to the Father." So we can end our quest right here, or can we? Jesus ascended into heaven forty days after His resurrection. Based on Christ's statement to Mary, no one would touch Him during this forty day time period — at least that is what this statement should mean. Right?

We know that this is not true. Consider a week later, Thomas, who missed the first encounter in the Upper Room, is ordered by Christ to place his hands in Jesus' wounds. How could Thomas refrain from embracing Christ and weeping tears of joy and love as he cried out, "My Lord and my God!"

When faced with this event, we come back to our starting point. Why was Mary denied the opportunity to do what others were permitted during the period between the resurrection and Christ's ascension into heaven, forty days later?

The answer to this question lies in the understanding of the Jewish ritual of atonement for sin on Yom Kippur. After the High Priest had slain the sin sacrifice, he took the blood and made his way to the Holy Place, stopping at the Bronze Laver to wash his hands and his feet. This was a requirement because, although the priest was consecrated, his feet had been exposed to the dirt of the courtyard, and his hands had been contaminated by handling the sacrifice. Once the priest washed this exposure to the sinful world from his hands and his feet, he could enter into God's dwelling place. Once he passed through the embroidered curtain, gaining access to the Holy Place, he approached the great Veil, blocking access to the Holy of Holies. Standing here before the Veil, the High Priest had other priests tie a rope to his leg. Should he fail to perform this ritual exactly as prescribed, or should the sacrifice be found unsatisfactory, the High Priest could very well be struck dead. In this event, the rope would be the only way to recover his body.

With fear and trembling, the High Priest would pass behind the Veil and approach the Mercy Seat sitting on top of the Ark of the Covenant. Standing before the very throne of God on earth, the High Priest would sprinkle the blood from the sin offering between the Cherubim with their outstretched wings. This alone was God's method for temporarily putting away the sins of the Jewish nation, God's people.

When God, Himself, passed this ritual to Moses, it was meant to be an earthly manifestation of a heavenly ritual. It looked forward to a future time when the perfect sin sacrifice would be made – once for all. We now read about that once future day. Christ has been the altar upon which the sacrifice was placed. He, without blemish, has served as the sin offering. He has spent the three days in the grave and is now resurrected. Think of where we find ourselves in the ritual described above. As the sun rises, do we not see that Christ is now the High Priest standing at the Brazen Altar, holding the blood of the perfect sin sacrifice (his own blood).

As Mary recognizes Him and approaches to embrace Him, He warns her off. "Don't embrace me, for I have not yet ascended to the Father." Christ is expressing His current role as High Priest. He is sanctified and consecrated. Mary's embrace would defile Him so that He could not enter into God's holy presence.

To fulfill the ritual given by God to Moses, Christ would ascend into heaven. Once there, He would enter into the heavenly Holy of Holies and approach the heavenly Mercy Seat. Here, He would sprinkle His precious blood, shed for all believers, completing the mysterious and blessed act of redemption. Once this work was completed, Christ returned to earth to prepare His disciples to lead the church. It is after the completion this ritual and His return to earth, that those who knew and loved Him are allowed to embrace him as Mary desired to do in the garden on Resurrection morning.

So in this most interesting encounter of the Easter story, we can now feel comfortable that we have an explanation for the rebuff of Mary. Jesus as our High Priest was consecrated and could not be embraced prior to His entering into the heavenly Holy of Holies. In the time between His encounter with Mary and His meeting of the two on the road to Emmaus, Jesus did ascend to the Father, and complete the ritual of atonement as it had been described to Moses.

Prayer: Thank you, Father, that Christ was faithful in His role as our High Priest to complete the prescribed ritual of atonement. Because of His faithfulness, we can know forgiveness for all of our sins. Thank you for His faithfulness in communicating this information to us. We rejoice in the fact that we have a High Priest who is able to atone for all of our sins and to restore us to a position of righteousness in God's sight.

REFERENCE

Definition of Yom Kippur retrieved from
    http://www.shalomnyc.org/feasts/yom_kippur.htm
Maynard, Jill (ed), The Illustrated Dictionary of Bible Life and Times, Readers'
    Digest, Pleasantville, NY, 1997

LESSON 11 NOTES:

LESSON 12 – Why did God Add John's Post Script?

Definition

Restoration: The act of returning a person to the place of standing he or she once held. The act of restoration implies the return to full authority and position without any limitation based on past acts or failures. In the Christian faith, restoration is exemplified in the passage from Psalms 103:12 "As far as the east is from the west, so far hath he removed our transgressions from us." If you consider a globe of the earth, if you start traveling north, you will eventually come to the pole and your travels will then be to the south. However, if you start traveling in an easterly direction, you will always travel east and will never be traveling west. This passage shows us the meaning of Christ restoring us by separating us completely from our sins.

Culture

Fishing was an important occupation during biblical times, and some enterprises thrived on the Sea of Galilee. Fishing was hard work.   Fishermen hauled and mended heavy nets, rowed cumbersome wooden boats, and sorted and prepared their catch for transport to distant markets, often working through the night. They used the dragnet – a large, weighted net thrown from the boat and then dragged toward shore, sometimes with the help of another crew. This method was used at night when the cooling waters drew fish to the surface.

A Fitting End to the Book

Let's look at John 20:30-31:

> Now Jesus did many other signs in the presence of the disciples, which are not written in this book; but these are written so that you may believe that Jesus is the Christ, the Son of God, and that by believing you may have life in his name.

So, the Disciple, whom Jesus loved, closes his Gospel story. It is a fitting end to the story. Then we turn the page and find John 21, a story of a final meeting of half of the disciples with Jesus at the Sea of Galilee. This chapter from the Gospel of John does read like a post script. It has the feel of being added as an afterthought. *Why?* This passage deals with some unfinished business. Here, we see recorded the face to face meeting between the resurrected Jesus and His disciple, Peter after Peter's famous denial. Let's see what happened:

> John 21:15-19 When they had finished breakfast, Jesus said to Simon Peter, "Simon, son of John, do you love me more than these?" He said to him, "Yes, Lord; you know that I love you." He said to him, "Feed my lambs."
>
> He said to him a second time, "Simon, son of John, do you love me?" He said to him, "Yes, Lord; you know that I love you." He said to him, "Tend my sheep."
>
> He said to him the third time, "Simon, son of John, do you love me?" Peter was grieved because he said to him the third time, "Do you love me?" and he said to him, "Lord, you know everything; you know that I love you." Jesus said to him, "Feed my sheep.

Truly, truly, I say to you, when you were young, you used to dress yourself and walk wherever you wanted, but when you are old, you will stretch out your hands, and another will dress you and carry you where you do not want to go." (This he said to show by what kind of death he was to glorify God.) And after saying this he said to him, "Follow me."

In John 18, we read about the events dealing with Peter's denial of Christ. At dinner, Peter proudly vowed that he would stand with Jesus and never deny Him. And then, in the courtyard of Caiaphas' house, Peter hears the cock crow immediately after making his third denial of knowing his Lord. In Luke's Gospel, we see that in that moment of the cock crowing, "the Lord turned and looked straight at Peter."

Peter had always been the leader of the group of twelve. Christ had focused on preparing him for this position. The other disciples followed his lead with little or no questioning. After his denial of Christ, we see very little of Peter. He is noticeably absent from the crucifixion and burial of Jesus. When he visits the empty tomb, Luke says he just turned away. Surely, the other disciples knew about Peter's denial. Then, in the book of Acts of the Apostles, we have Peter, once again, providing the leadership for the disciples and the young church.

Somehow, the other disciples had their faith in Peter as their leader restored. **Why this change in Peter?** Without this final chapter from John, we would be left in the dark; because he added it to his gospel, we can see what happened to change Peter.

Let's take a look at this transforming event in Peter's life. Five men, disciples of Christ, spend the night fishing. Can you imagine the stories they told – of their first fishing trip as boys, the whopper that got away and, more than likely, the events of the past three years. They know that Jesus is alive. They have met with Him. They have touched Him and eaten with Him. See Peter, somewhat withdrawn, still struggling with the "demons" within, remembering the events of the past three years, but always coming back to that single moment – the roster's crow – and the eyes of Christ upon him! Every time his heart starts to warm, every time hope starts to form – the idea that perhaps he could find forgiveness, the voice within him cries out "No! No! You denied Him! There can be no hope for you!"

What a night for Peter! Jesus knows our hurts. He brings light to the darkest corners of our heart. And as the night of unsuccessful fishing draws to a close with the first rays of dawn's light, Christ comes to Peter and the others.

In an event reliving an experience of Jesus' early ministry, he tells these unsuccessful fishermen to drop their nets on the other side of the boat. And just as in the earlier event, they pull their nets in full of fish. In this act, Jesus reconfirms their call to be fishers of men.

What follows is a series of events as reported by John. They are very significant to our understanding of Peter… and ourselves. It is most commonly believed that Peter was excited, even anxious to see Jesus. However, it is more likely that Peter is caught in the grips of his guilt. He wants to clear the air with Jesus, something that can only be done face-to-face; and he feels unworthy of coming to Jesus, face-to-face. This tension between what he knows he has to do and what his guilt prevents him from doing drive the sequence of events which follow.

Let's step through the highlights of the events:

Peter is stripped down to work with the nets. He hears that Jesus is on the beach, one hundred yards away. He wraps his heavy cloak around himself to swim to shore. Peter is obviously a strong swimmer. But in this event, swimming against a boat being rowed by four fishermen, it is entirely possible that they beat Peter, swimming in his heavy, water-logged cloak, to shore.

Jesus, who already has bread and fish cooked, asks for more fish. Normally, the youngest of the group would do this task. Someone goes for the fish, but ends up counting the number caught (153) and inspecting all of the nets. My gut feeling is that it was Peter who did this.

Finally, Peter can find nothing else to do and his face-to-face meeting with Christ occurs and we hear a very cryptic exchange. Three times, Christ asks Peter if he loves Him. Three times, Peter says, "Lord, you know I love you." Christ then tells Peter to "feed My sheep". **Why** is Peter sad when Christ asks him this question the third time? This just does not make sense.

The answer lies in the language. The Greek of the New Testament has several different words for love. God selected the languages of the Old and New Testaments because of the ability of the languages to communicate clearly. Let's examine two different words for love.

First, we have the word *agape*. This word is often translated as godly love – to love as God loves. A second word for love is phileo or brotherly love. We get the name Philadelphia (City of Brotherly Love) from this Greek word. Phileo is often translated as "like" or "fond of". With this additional information, let's look at this exchange between Peter and Jesus, considering the Greek words used. The first exchange reads like this:

> When they had finished eating, Jesus said to Simon Peter, "Simon son of John, do you love (*agape*) me *with God's love* more than these?"
>
> "Yes, Lord," he said, "you know that I like (*phileo*) you."
>
> Jesus said, "Feed my lambs

The second exchange was just like it.

> Again Jesus said, "Simon son of John, do you truly love (*agape*) me with God's love?" He answered, "Yes, Lord, you know that I like (*phileo*) you." Jesus said, "Take care of my sheep."

The third exchange between Peter and Jesus is different.

> The third time he said to him, "Simon son of John, do you like (*phileo*) me?"
>
> **Peter was hurt** because Jesus asked him the third time, "Do you like (*phileo*) me?" He said, "Lord, you know all things; you know that I like (*phileo*) you."
>
> Jesus said, "Feed my sheep."

Do you see it, now? Peter's hurt comes from the change in Jesus' question. As we see Peter face to face with Christ for apparently the first time since his denial, we see Jesus extending full forgiveness and restoration to Peter. The question by Christ is more of a statement that Peter can be restored to full fellowship with Christ. Despite his act of denial, Peter can know and experience the fullness of God's agape love.

Peter's response comes truly from his heart. Recognizing what he did by denying Christ, Peter cannot say in clear conscience that he truly loves Christ with God's agape love. He responds by saying "Lord, you know I like you." Christ responds by telling Peter to reassume his place of leadership by feeding Christ's sheep.

Christ tries once again to let Peter know that full restoration is available to him. Jesus questions Peter a second time. Peter, still holding on to his guilt, replies, "Lord, you know I really like you."

On the third exchange, Christ having extended full restoration, now meets Peter in his honesty where he really is. Christ asks," Peter do you really like me?" Christ has come down to Peter's level to meet him. Christ *always* desires us to be where He wants us to be – but He also *always* meets us where we are. Peter is saddened by the change in Christ's question, but recognizes that Christ still extends to him the command to lead.

Then Jesus prophesies over Peter:

> Truly, truly, I say to you, when you were young, you used to dress yourself and walk wherever you wanted, but when you are old, you will stretch out your hands, and another will dress you and carry you where you do not want to go." (This he said to show by what kind of death he was to glorify God.) And after saying this he said to him, "Follow me."

In this revelation, Peter sees that he is restored to his position of leadership in the presence of the other disciples. They also hear

- 125-

Christ reconfirm Peter's leadership role. If you can remember when there has been a rift among friends, the relief and joy that comes when the rift is healed and fellowship restored. No longer do the friends have to walk around as on eggshells. This is probably the feeling running through this group of disciples.

Admire Peter in his honesty. A lesser man might have been tempted to say, "Yes, Lord, I agape you!" Peter is too honest to grab this easy out. He knows in his heart that his faith is not there. In the moment of testing, he failed Christ. But the Bible is true ... in our weakness, He perfects our strength.

I cannot help but believe that years later, as Peter walks out to be crucified upside down, he is saying, "Lord, you know I agape you!"

So we have a post script from John. In this special story, we see that even though we might be reluctant to come to Jesus with our failures and denials, He stands ready to forgive and restore. We can see that His restoration returns us to a place of usefulness. In the case of Peter, we see restoration contributing to the successful planting of the church.

Prayer: Thank you, Jesus, that You are patient with us while we swim to shore and count fish and inspect nets. You wait patiently for us to meet You face-to-face. Thank you for the gift of restoration. We pray that, as Peter learned to say, so we will also be able to say, Lord you know I really love you!

REFERENCE

Maynard, Jill (ed.),The Illustrated Dictionary of Bible Life and Times, Readers' Digest, Pleasantville, NY, 1997

LESSON 12 NOTES:

About the Authors

Tim Cummings declares himself to be an *evangelist to business owners*. As an experienced businessman and an accredited mentor he assists CEOs and Entrepreneurs to speak out the vision for his or her businesses and then aides in the execution of that vision in proper sequence. He counsels Christian business people to accept that they *are* engaged in full time ministry when working in their businesses as God has given them resources and authority to bring Christ to the market place on a daily basis!

Tim has always had a hunger to know God better and to understand His love letter more. He enjoys seeing other Christians grow in their faith as they learn to trust the historical accuracy of the Bible and to experience the love of their Heavenly Father. He is an advocate of critical thinking, a skill which serves Christians well as we are called to be transformed by the renewal of our minds! A native of Tennessee, he continues to reside in Nashville.

LGC is Tim's youngest child and what he lovingly refers to as a renaissance woman. She loves God and has been gifted by Him as a writer and artist. Because of her writing skills, Tim picked her, at age 13, to take his teachings and redraft them for pre-teens and teenagers.

She has grown up in Nashville, Tennessee and currently resides in New York City while attending college.

CPSIA information can be obtained at www.ICGtesting.com
Printed in the USA
LVOW091154220212

269917LV00001B/28/P

9 780983 000365